MW01531610

FAMOUS
ISN'T ENOUGH:

EARNING YOUR FORTUNE AS AN ENTREPRENEUR

Judy Hoberman

FAMOUS ISN'T ENOUGH: EARNING YOUR
FORTUNE AS AN ENTREPRENEUR

FAMOUS ISN'T ENOUGH: EARNING YOUR FORTUNE AS AN ENTREPRENEUR

TABLE OF CONTENTS

FAMOUS ISN'T ENOUGH: EARNING YOUR FORTUNE AS AN ENTREPRENEUR

ACKNOWLEDGEMENTS

Throughout my years on this wonderful earth, I have been fortunate to have met, been surrounded by and given birth to some amazing people. It always surprises me (and yet it doesn't surprise me at all) whom I can trust, whom I should be wary of, and who has my back, no matter what.

This book is for all of those people who trust in me, who have my back, and who are good right down to their bones.

I will start with the obvious: my children. When I first began my journey into entrepreneurship, my loving son PJ was the one who showed me what I couldn't see— that I had something to say. He had to talk me off the ledge more than once, and if you ever need an intelligent, loving and handsome old soul in your corner, he's the one you want. I am so grateful for all the lessons learned from my young son.

And then there is my first born, my beautiful baby girl Stephanie. She is the joy and the light of my life (although we did have to navigate through those wonderful mother-daughter years of growth). She is my cheerleader, my promoter and my mini-me. I see the younger me in her, and when people tell me what an outstanding woman she is, my buttons pop with pride. I know and she knows that if we had to get to each other, nothing could stand in our way.

To all my friends that always believed that I can do whatever it takes to be a successful entrepreneur and role model, this book is dedicated to you. Having you at the other end of the phone or email or Skype call means the world to me.

Jason Markow and Leslie Thompson, I need to lump you together because you complement each other brilliantly in handling all of my marketing efforts and putting together the pieces of the puzzle to share my story. Many years ago, a blind date asked me what I brought to the table. I said, "I bring the table." That is what you two bring to my world. How would I be able to finish this book in record time if not for your encouragement and expertise?

To my new family of Taylors, I love you all and thank you for accepting me as me! You have seen me as the crazy New Yorker trying to fit into your Texas world, and I hope you also have seen that nothing matters more to me than family. My two new daughters, Alena and Megan, were the bonus prize for me.

And, finally, my deepest thanks to my husband Don, aka The Colonel. Our strategizing, although painful to me at times, is really what keeps me focused and on target. You get me, you see me, and you love me—you really love me—and that just keeps me going. (Now if we could only figure out a way to have one place of residence, that would be the icing on the cake.) Thank you for believing in what I do and not telling me to change my path, even when it seemed to be the right thing to say. This Skirt loves her Colonel.

I am blessed to have so many wonderful people around me that bring joy, happiness, and some much needed balance.

Famous Isn't Enough is not necessarily about having your name in lights. It's more about following your passion and having those that believe in you surround you and encourage you. I have that, and I couldn't be happier.

FAMOUS ISN'T ENOUGH: EARNING YOUR FORTUNE AS AN ENTREPRENEUR

FOREWORD

Everything about Judy says "RADICAL" to me. Not just because she raised two amazing children as a single mom. Not just because she built a stellar corporate career. And not just because she left that corporate job to start her own business.

She's RADICAL because she's committed to following her own passion and dreams and then sharing that journey with others—to inspire, educate and inform. Her desire to open up and show people the ups and downs of starting and growing a business speaks to her authentic aspiration to help you avoid some of the missteps and mistakes she's made. It also shows her willingness to let you in on the processes, strategies and methods that absolutely worked.

I met Judy when she attended my Get RADICAL Women's Conference several years ago. At a crossroads, she longed for a change—something more, something different. It was during that event that she made a radical decision about the direction of her life—to leave her corporate career and embark on the very winding road called entrepreneurship.

I was honored to be Judy's Business Coach as she transitioned from her corporate job to business owner. And what I know is that she is smart, tenacious, focused and determined—not just so she can reach her own goals, but so she can help others do the same.

That's what this book is all about. Judy has, through her own experiences and in talking with other successful business owners, crafted a blueprint for being able to have the business you want—the one that generates revenue, allows time for your family and doesn't leave out the time for self-care. She's giving you powerful "lessons learned," so you can avoid pitfalls and attain results faster.

In this age of the Internet, technology and an abundance of information, it can be hard to sift through the noise—to know where to go to get the right information. This book brings to the forefront, from those who have been there, what it takes to really build the business of your dreams.

I have watched Judy establish a thriving, prosperous business while having a generous heart and strong desire to help others to the same. I'm proud to know her and can't wait to see what she does next.

Doreen Rainey
CEO, RADICAL Success Institute

INTRODUCTION

Little more than 50 years ago, the ideal career path in America looked very different than it does today. Young people dreamt of graduating college and landing a job with a stable company—a company in which they could put down roots and build their career over two or three decades. They longed for the certainty of punching the clock, doing the same routine year in and year out, and earning a gold watch and a comfortable pension for retirement.

Oh, but times have changed! Today, the American Dream for many is one filled with risk and uncertainty. A dream built on independence and ingenuity. It is the dream of entrepreneurship—one that I have long cherished.

When I first decided to create a new business,

admittedly I had delusions of grandeur. I come from a world where you don't give up and failure is not an option. No, I didn't grow up like that; I created that world. It may have seemed like a fantasy world to many, but it worked for me.

Other than two years in my professional life, I have always been self-employed, working as an independent contractor on straight commission. I'm a hard worker and definitely believe in myself and in my abilities. I always knew that I wouldn't starve, because I could just work a little harder if I needed something. But, it wasn't just me that I had to worry about. For the first half of my career, I was balancing my work life with the responsibilities of a single mom raising two amazing children. Although having the kids at home meant I had to earn enough to support the three of us, they also helped me set and achieve goals that were higher than those I might have set for just myself.

For example, the very first time the three of us went on vacation together, back in the '90s, I let the kids choose where they wanted to go. Think they wanted a "stay-cation" with mom? Fat chance. They chose Aruba. Once I figured out the flights, hotel, and everything else, it was turning into a pricey trip. I didn't want to have credit card bills for months after, so I made a goal to earn enough extra money before we left to pay for the entire trip—and I did. It was a wonderful vacation, and an even better experience knowing that we came home to zero extra bills.

That's basically my M.O. If I need something, I get it done. And that's been true for most of my adult life. Then, I took a detour in my career and accepted a position as a Senior Director in Corporate America, for which I earned a bi-weekly paycheck. What a weird concept. If you worked more or harder, you didn't get rewarded. If you worked less or did nothing, you didn't lose your earnings. How was this possible? Why did anyone want someone else to dictate what they were worth and when they had to work and whether they could take time off, or forbid them from watching their child's sporting event? That type of regimented structure, along with the typical workplace drama, soon led to my resignation. (You can read all of the intriguing details in my blog, www.growthisoptional.com.)

So, there I was, unemployed and having to start all over...again! The kids were grown and out of the house at this point, and so I was truly fending for myself. My head was swimming with questions, and for the first time, I experienced self-doubt. What do I do? How do I do it? What will bring in revenue? How do I decide what I want to be when I grow up?

In my case, I found a business coach who helped lead me on the right path. I will get into the merits of a good coach later in this book, but my overriding goal is to help you lay the foundation for those conversations.

Although I have worked as an independent contractor for nearly my entire career, I did not fully embrace entrepreneurship until just a few years ago. *Famous Isn't Enough: Earning Your Fortune as an Entrepreneur* is the story of the lessons I have learned along the journey. I will tell you the good, the bad, the better and the worse. I'll give you tips and ideas, and I will also tell you very frankly what not to do. Some of you will do those things anyway. And that's okay, because sometimes you have to experience something yourself to really understand. Just make sure you learn the lesson, so you can share your wisdom with other budding entrepreneurs down the road.

As part of my research for the book, I asked several dozen friends and associates what they would like to know if they were starting a business today. It's the old "if I knew then what I know now" theory. Their invaluable wisdom is documented throughout these pages, as well.

And so, read on! Enjoy, learn, implement, and succeed in earning a living as an entrepreneur—whether or not you ever want to be famous!

CHAPTER ONE

TAKE THE PLUNGE

What gives you the push to start a business? Have you always wanted to be the CEO of your own company? Do you have an idea that you want to share with the world? Or perhaps, you are simply so unhappy where you are in your life that a radical change seems the only logical solution.

In my case, I was looking at Door Number 3. I knew I was not where I was supposed to be in my life. I knew I wanted something more, but I wasn't sure what it was. I also knew I was miserable where I was, but didn't know what would make me happy. And finally, I knew that if I didn't do something soon, I would repeat past behaviors and continue to stay stuck.

What would any normal person do if they found themselves in this predicament? Start a business, of course! Being self-employed sounds great on the surface—and, in many ways, it is the best career imaginable. But, what really happens when you take the plunge, and how can you ensure that you will swim, not sink, as a business owner?

Throughout this book, we will explore a myriad of questions, considerations and strategies to help you determine whether entrepreneurship is for you, and formulate a game plan for success if you decide to take the plunge. I encourage you to keep a journal or notepad close at hand, so that you can jot down ideas and thoughts that come to mind. You may find yourself reflecting about past choices you have made, as well as the skills and passions that can take you where you want to go. No matter where you end up, your journal will provide you with greater clarity for the decisions you make along the way.

Make a Choice
Few people begin their professional career as an entrepreneur; rather, they learn their craft working for one or several employers before deciding to strike out on their own. The wonderful thing about entrepreneurship, though, is that it is open to anyone. Whether you are only a few years into your career or a seasoned executive, you can create your own venture. Likewise, whether you work in manufacturing, logistics, technology, hospitality, or any other industry, you can choose to be independent and set up shop for yourself.

My entire professional career has been in sales. I have worked in a variety of industries, from roofing to burglar alarms, and ultimately the insurance world. Although sales was, and still is, a male-dominated field, I continually excelled as a woman, nailing my quotas, breaking records and winning countless awards. Ironically, the secret to my success was the fact that I very purposefully did the opposite of what my male peers did (and my male trainers taught). I approached sales from a woman's perspective and focused on building relationships rather than the transactional way of doing business, which is get in, get out and get the check. Those relationships led to referrals, and throughout most of my career, I never had to make cold calls or beg for leads.

My one detour from a commission-based livelihood was a two-year stint in Corporate America as a Senior Director working in sales training. I had a cushy office and a cushy salary, but I was desperately unhappy. It's funny, because whenever I talk about my "time" in corporate, I make it sound like it was a death sentence. It wasn't. Well, not really, at least not all the time. But, ultimately, I came to realize that I have always been and always will be an entrepreneur. I am happiest when I have the freedom to do and be whatever I want. I spent 30 years in sales as a 1099 independent contractor, choosing positions that gave me the freedom to earn what I wanted and the flexibility to spend time with my children. Coming into the corporate arena was a new phenomenon, and I had never experienced anything like it. As a commission-based sales person, if you didn't sell, you didn't earn. You had a lot of flexibility, but you also had to deliver the goods, or you would go hungry. In corporate, you got paid whether you did a stellar job or a mediocre job. There was no incentive to exceed expectations, because you got a check either way.

Also, in corporate, you had regular hours. In by 8:00 a.m. and out by 5:00 p.m. You didn't need a watch because you could see the mass exodus leaving the building the minute the workday was officially done and the clock-punchers rolling in at 8 o'clock sharp the next morning. Again, the whole regimen was new to me.

All of the departments worked in silos. I had heard that before, but until you really experience it, you can't believe it. For instance, as trainers, our task was to build training for a new product. We needed to understand how the product worked and paid—this was insurance, after all. So, we would meet with the actuaries and they would explain how the plan was designed so that there would be a profit. Then, we would have a separate meeting with the Claims Department, so they could explain how the plan pays. We also had meetings with Billing, IT, Legal, and so on, but no two departments were ever in the same room at the same time. Consequently, the entire process was riddled with inefficiency. We would talk to the product developers and have our training outline in mind. Next, the actuaries would come in and give us their point of view, which didn't necessarily ring true with the developers, so we would "adjust" the training until Claims came in and made us re-adjust everything again. To me, the separate meetings were a waste of everyone's time, but no one wanted to rock the boat and make changes.

I do believe that many people are well suited for corporate careers. My husband loves the stability, and many of my friends wouldn't work anywhere else. I did enjoy a steady paycheck, but I felt like I was off my game. I was the proverbial square peg in a round hole. Ultimately, some people are made to be entrepreneurs and some are not. When you try to force yourself into one role or another, unless it fits, don't waste years of your life trying to be like everyone else. As the saying goes, "Stop trying to fit in when you were born to stand out."

After two years of playing nicely and getting things done as best as possible, I decided to dive headfirst back into what I knew best. Welcome to the world of being an entrepreneur!

Dream a Little Dream

To pursue a career path that is fraught with risk and uncertainty takes a certain kind of moxie. Passion and motivation are fundamental building blocks for success. As you start to formulate a vision of your life as an entrepreneur, consider journaling about these three questions:

1. **If you could do anything you wanted and you could not fail, what would you be doing?** Imagine that time, age and money were not obstacles—there are no limits, just possibilities. This is where our dreams begin. You have to start at the end and work your way backward. Be daring and stretch yourself!

2. **Where do you see yourself in 24 months?** We all know how quickly time flies, and two years will pass before you know it. What is your picture?

Where are you? Are you living your passion? Have you fulfilled your dream? Write your answer as if you are living it now, using the present tense. (If you can't see it, how can it happen?)

3. **What are you going to do next?** If you are doing what you love to do right now and that is your calling, what can you add to your life to make it extraordinary? It's easier to accomplish the impossible than the ordinary. Is it scary to think about your dreams? Then you are on to something big!

Starting a business is a tremendous leap of faith. You have to trust that others want and need what you have to offer. More importantly, you have to trust that you have the talent and skill to deliver your products or services with excellence. (After all, nobody ever set out to start a business that delivers so-so customer service.) As you begin to formulate the concept for your venture, think big—huge, even. Let the vision of a future thriving enterprise fuel your confidence to take that first big step.

Put Up Your Dukes
Of course, as soon as you announce your intention to leave the traditional workforce, any number of people will feel obligated to tell you that you're crazy, that your idea won't sell, and that you should have a real job, not a hobby. They might even use convoluted logic to throw you off your game, telling you that you can't be successful, because you don't have experience doing what you want

to do, and you can't get the experience, because you have to be successful to make things happen.

Sound familiar? Everyone has those naysayers around them, and you either listen or you don't. I stopped listening to the pessimists early on and made a point of seeking out people who offered support and encouragement for my endeavors. One of my favorite quotes comes from the legendary physicist Albert Einstein, who said, "The only source of knowledge is experience." What better way to get experience than to create a job that is custom tailored to your skills and your passions?

Even so, taking the plunge into entrepreneurship can be scary. You may find inspiration in the following excerpt from a 2005 Commencement address at Stanford University given by the late Steve Jobs, the legendary CEO of Apple:

> "You've got to find what you love, and that is as true for work as it is for your lovers. Your work is going to fill a large part of your life, and the only way to be truly satisfied is to do what you believe is great work, and the only way to do great work is to love what you do. If you haven't found it yet, keep looking, and don't settle. As with all matters of the heart, you'll know when you find it, and like any great relationship it just gets better and better as the years roll on. So keep looking. Don't settle."

> "...Don't let the noise of others' opinions

drown out your own inner voice, heart and intuition. They somehow already know what you truly want to become. Everything else is secondary."

Pursue Your Passion

When you think of starting a business, it only makes sense to do something that you know. If you are an engineer, you probably don't want to start a crafts business. If you are a talented graphic designer, you might not want to embark on a new career in SEO consulting. Get my drift?

When I decided to start my own company, I asked myself several questions to help me define my focus. These questions may help guide your thought process, as well:

- What do I know the best?

- What could I do that would help people?

- What unique insights do I have to offer?

- What makes me an expert?

- What do I really *care* about?

The last question is the most critical. You may excel at something and have unique insights to offer, but if you are not passionate about the work, then you are destined to fail. Building a business takes sweat equity—in the beginning, you will be filling multiple roles as you get your venture off the ground. Your passion for the work gives you the motivation to get started early every day (when no one else is holding you accountable) and provides the fuel that keeps you going through the ups and downs.

As I reflected on each of the questions myself, the answers helped guide me toward the goal of striking out on my own. Since I had worked in sales for nearly three decades, the answer to the first question was obvious: I know sales. As a corollary, I know people, and I know how to communicate. Is there one area in which you have extensive experience? Have you studied a particular niche or practiced a talent longer than most? Targeting the subject matter that you know best will help you stand out from the masses.

What is the vision that keeps you up at night, the idea you can't get out of your head? Consider how you can use your passion to solve a problem for other people, and you have found your new business.

Now, let's go a little further. Do you need any designations or specialized training or extra schooling to pursue your desired venture? If so, how long will it take to get these in place? In my case, I've had training, built training, and even facilitated training. I knew I wanted to focus on sales, but I would not need an industry-specific degree or certification for the type of business that I envisioned. So far, so good.

Next, you have to ask yourself: Is there a need? In other words, can you make money doing what you are planning to do? If you are launching your own business, it not only needs to be something you know about and are passionate about, but also something others need to have. Often, this is the biggest gap in the plan.

If you determine that there is a need for the product or service you will be offering, is it something that people need all the time, just during certain seasons, only when the economy is good, or when the economy is not so strong? In short, you should know what conditions are necessary for you to have a viable business. The existence or absence of those conditions will determine whether or not you can actually earn a living.

Likewise, there may be a strong need for what you have to offer, but the marketplace may also be crowded with competitors. Looking for ways to narrow the scope of your services or specialize in a smaller market can help you meet the needs of a particular group while differentiating yourself from your competitors. We'll talk about carving out a niche in a later chapter.

Ultimately, you should do a lot of soul-searching before starting a business. Is it something you have been dreaming about and talking about for months or even years? Has the idea been keeping you up at night? Or did one of your friends start a business, and you figured they're making money and it looks like fun? You need to be honest here. Starting a business is no easy task, and it isn't a hobby. Let me say that again: it is not a hobby! You will be spending vast amounts of your time, your energy, your family's time, and your money on getting your business off the ground. So please, before you cut the ribbon and join the Chamber, be really sure this is what you want. Remember the saying, "Do what you love, and love what you do." You don't want to fail this test, and it's not graded on a curve.

The following self-assessment may help you feel more confident in your decision. The test is meant to help gauge whether you possess the character traits and fundamental skills needed for success as an entrepreneur, and whether you have a strong support system in place. This is not meant to be an exact evaluation, but rather give you an idea of how well suited you are to the life of an entrepreneur.

ENTREPRENEUR SELF ASSESSMENT

YES   NO

_____ _____ 1. Are you generally optimistic, even when faced with a difficult situation?

_____ _____ 2. Do you stay focused until a task is completed?

_____ _____ 3. Do you think creatively when trying to solve a problem?

_____ _____ 4. Can you make quick decisions?

_____ _____ 5. Are you adaptable to change?

_____ _____ 6. Can you motivate yourself, instead of relying on others for direction and deadlines?

_____ _____ 7. Do you enjoy competition?

_____ _____ 8. Do you have good organizational skills?

_____ _____ 9. Do you have experience as a manager or supervisor?

_____ _____ 10. Are you a good listener?

_____ _____ 11. Are you willing to work long hours and forgo weekend activities and vacations to get your business off the ground?

YES   NO

_____   _____   12. Do you understand the basics of a balance sheet and income statement?

_____   _____   13. Have you ever put together or managed a budget?

_____   _____   14. Would your family and friends be supportive of your decision to work for yourself?

_____   _____   15. Are you willing to network and reach out to others for guidance and information?

If you have at least nine "yes" answers, you have the potential to be successful with your new business venture. If you answered fewer than nine questions positively, consider whether you can find a business partner, hire an employee, or find additional resources to fill in the gaps.

Get a Coach

When I first began working on the outline for this book, I asked a number of professionals a simple question: If you were deciding to start a business, what is the one thing you wish you knew? The overwhelming response was, "I wish I had a coach."

If you have never worked with a business coach, you might wonder why having a coach is such a big deal. Simply put, a coach can take your idea and put it on steroids. As the saying goes, if you want to be good at something you do it alone; if you want to be great, you get a coach.

I didn't know that I needed a coach when I first started out as an entrepreneur and was very fortunate that one practically fell in my lap. I had received an email for a conference in the Washington, DC area about "getting radical" in your life. As a child of the '60s, images of protests and sit-ins immediately came to mind, which is perhaps why this particular email caught my eye.

Although I was intrigued, I was not yet committed, so I called my sister-in-law in New Jersey and suggested we meet at the conference. It was halfway between New Jersey and Texas, where I lived, and I figured if the content didn't strike a chord with us, we could leave and just hang out together for the weekend. As it turned out, the conference totally rocked my world. The featured presenter, Doreen Rainey, was both inspiring and insightful; she made you think about yourself and your life's goals. I hung on her every word. My "radical" event happened the day I returned from the conference, when I promptly handed in my resignation at my corporate job. I met with Doreen one-on-one the day after my last day of work, and my journey to entrepreneurship got the kick-start it needed.

The fundamental question that Doreen continually asked was, "If you could do anything you wanted and money, time and age were not a factor—and you *could not* fail—what would that be?" The answer was at once easy and very difficult. I knew what I wanted to do, but I wasn't sure of myself.

Did I have it in me one more time to start a business? To grow it from nothing? To get out there with no support from anyone in my local area? To dream bigger than I was prepared to do? What does that process look like? And, when all is said and done, will anyone other than me really care?

Step by step, and page by page, Doreen and I created a road map to the next chapter of my life. It was hard work and I went through lots of tissues, but she was instrumental in helping me define my company. As a budding entrepreneur, you likely have an independent spirit and may be disinclined to ask for input. You may be concerned that a coach won't share your passion, or will lead you down the wrong path. You may want to save the money. From my own experience, I can tell you that hiring a business coach dramatically increased my chances of success as I launched my business and delivered an outstanding return on my investment. Not only did I have an ally in my corner to help me through the emotional challenges of entrepreneurship, but I had wise counsel from a business expert who could help me think strategically about the marketplace and creating my brand. Still not convinced? Just remember, even Peyton Manning has a coach.

Get it in Gear

After several sessions with Doreen, I decided my business would be sales training with a slight twist—I would help women, I would help men, and I would help them work together. I've done that my entire life, I figured, so how hard could it be to make it the focus of my services? I even picked a clever name for my new consulting business: Selling in a Skirt.

Whenever you start a business, you have to have an unforgettable brand, something that people will remember. Many people want it to be their own name and build a legacy with their name. That wasn't what I wanted to do.

I wrote down everything I could think of that had to do with sales and women. After wracking my brain for several hours, I looked at my notepad and had nothing— none of my ideas had the "wow factor." Frustrated, I took a fresh start and tried to think of something that described not just what I did, but what I wanted to do, what I wanted to accomplish with my business. I came up with Selling in a Skirt, because it describes what I wanted to help women do—sell as women, communicate as women, and still be women. Of course, the comment I get the most from men is that they don't wear a skirt. My response is, "You don't have to wear one, you just have to think like one, and more importantly, understand one." The next comment is usually, "Makes perfect sense. Tell me more."

Going back to my list of questions, I had decades of experience and training, so I knew I had unique insights and qualified as an expert. I also knew there was a need, because I lived it. In addition, through my networking, I did my own market research and confirmed that there was a void in the market—no one was doing what I was planning to do.

Could I make money in sales training that focused on how men and women communicate? I was certain that if there were a need, people would pay to be taught. Sales training isn't a seasonal business. In fact, if you don't have a sales team, your business will not grow. Even if you are an attorney or CPA, you are still selling yourself. So, as to the questions of need and income, check and check.

Did I think about the economy? I knew it was not great, since so many layoffs were happening, but I never thought the flagging economy would affect sales and training. After all, companies won't thrive if they don't have sales. Sales bring revenue into a company, no matter what the economy is doing. (I would learn later that my logic was flawed. Sales are mandatory, training is optional. I'll share what I did to overcome this hurdle a little later in the book.)

Now the big question: WHY? Why would I want to start a business? Why wouldn't I just stay in a nice cushy position and bring in money every other week? Why would I want to have to prospect and sell my services? *Why?*

The real answer is that I love the challenge of creating something from nothing. I love the fact that I don't really have to answer to anyone but myself. I also love to help people and discover what makes them tick. I find it fascinating to discern why men and women do the things they do. When the light bulb goes on, I want to be the one flipping the switch. Do I need any other whys? I think I have them covered. The question is, do you?

Ready, Shoot, Aim

Of course, there is more to laying the foundation for a successful business start-up than just these few pieces. What about a business plan? The pundits all say you have to have one, and who am I to argue? Thanks to the wonders of the Internet, you can find examples online in a flash, do a little copy-and-paste, and your business plan is complete! Funny thing, though—I didn't even get that far. I was too busy telling people about my new venture to detail all the ins and outs of how it would operate. I had the vision and the mission on paper, and I had a general outline of my business structure, but the rest of my business plan was in my head. I chose to ignore the little matter of differentiating myself from the competition and putting together my entire marketing strategy and financial forecasts, figuring those minor details would work themselves out over time.

You're probably thinking, "Doesn't she know you have a better chance of succeeding when you write things down?" Yes, I'm a sales trainer—I talk about writing your goals down every day. So, in this case, do what I say, not what I do. (In other words, please learn from my mistakes.) When I first set out on my new path as an entrepreneur, I really didn't feel that a written business plan was necessary. Here was my reasoning:

1. I was in business for myself.

2. I was never going to have anyone else in the business.

3. I had an idea of what my business would look like.

4. I knew how much money I wanted to make.

5. Writing a business plan was a waste of time.

Doesn't each one of these reasons make perfect sense? They did for me, and later I will share just how easy it is to get off course if you don't have a roadmap to which you can refer. In short, take the time to put together a business plan. You may hate me now, but you'll thank me later. If you're not sure where to start, the Small Business Administration offers an excellent article series to guide you through the process at www.sba.gov. (Look in the Starting & Managing section of the website.)

> *To launch your business, you need a vision statement, a mission statement, and a business plan. You also need to think about money—where you get it and how to spend it.*

Do the Math

When I decided to become an entrepreneur, pursuing my passion was much more important than achieving a luxurious lifestyle. Even so, finances were an important consideration. People are in business to make money, bring value, and do what they love. You may not think the money comes first, but profits let you continue to do great things and make a difference in your field, or in society as a whole. You can give back and help those coming up the ranks become successful. Making money also makes you more credible in the eyes of your prospects and clients, providing assurance that you are someone who can achieve results. Here are few key questions to ask yourself as you address the financial side of your new venture, so you can reach your goals both personally and professionally:

1. **How much cash do you have to start your business?** You can interpret this question in two ways. First, how much money do you need to start your business? Second, how much money do you have to start your business? I had put away a

nice stash to start and operate my business. Even so, I did not factor how much time it would take to get a regular income stream, or how quickly I would go through my nest egg. These are key considerations, and I encourage you to sit down with your CPA or a business advisor who can help you with financial forecasting to ensure you don't run out of dough before you have cash flow coming in. Setting up your business structure in the right way is also critical, so be sure to meet with both your CPA and an attorney to discuss the pros and cons of operating as a sole proprietorship vs. a corporation in terms of taxes, expenses and legal safeguards.

2. **How will your business make money?** Have you done some market research? It doesn't have to be a formal focus group. It can be as simple as networking with the right group of people to see whether your idea is valid and valuable. Did you check out your competition to see what they are selling, what they are charging, and what they are doing wrong? Look at their websites and see what you love but, most importantly, what doesn't work for you. These gaps represent opportunities for you to position your business as a better solution and capture part of your competitors' market share. Look at how similar businesses are pricing their products and services, and put together a set of income goals

and projections based on the going rates.

3. **How will your business spend money?**
Will you have recurring monthly bills, such as
rent for office space or utilities? Will you be
shipping products on a regular basis? Do you
have to create materials for your clients? I didn't
give enough thought to this question when I first
launched my sales consulting business. I wanted
to make sure that I had everything I needed
and then some. In addition, I was and am very
particular about my look and my brand. I had
to make sure that I didn't dilute or compromise
that with poorly produced training materials.
Consequently, I went through my stash of cash
much faster than anticipated. Make sure you
write down everything, and I mean *everything,*
on which you might spend money. You may be
shocked to see what you will be spending, but
knowing your expenditures up front will allow
you to adjust your timeframe, pricing or budget
and keep you from flipping upside-down before
you even get started.

4. **How will your business make up cash shortages
during months with negative cash flow?**
Just when you think you've accounted for every
expense and you have it all planned out so you will
always have cash flow, remember that nothing
is guaranteed. I have had lucrative speaking

engagements rescheduled at the last minute and pre-booked training programs cancelled by a client. You have to plan for the best and prepare for the worst. That means making sure you have Plan B for your cash flow, if your business experiences an unexpected setback. Better to be safe than sorry.

Hopefully, you are now going through your checklist, whether mentally or (preferably) on paper. If you are shaking your head in disbelief and already think this is much too much work, you are right. If you are nodding your head thinking you've got this covered, you are also right. As the quintessential entrepreneur Henry Ford once said, "Whether you think you can, or you think you can't, you're right."

If, after all the soul searching and number crunching, you are ready to continue along on the journey, the next step is an important one. Most people have it down after a few iterations. Are you up for the challenge?

FAMOUS ISN'T ENOUGH: EARNING YOUR FORTUNE AS AN ENTREPRENEUR

CHAPTER TWO

KNOW YOUR TARGET

To be successful in business, you need clients. Seems such an obvious statement, but so many aspiring entrepreneurs fail to give serious consideration to their target audience.

Can you describe your perfect client? I'm talking about in great detail, with nothing left to the imagination. How do you do that?

If it takes too long to describe your ideal client, you are still not clear about who that is—a common problem among entrepreneurs. If you ask some would-be business owners who their ideal client is, they will say, "Everyone." Of course, that can't be true. Not everyone needs everything or anything. (Truth be told, women are the worst at this. Why? Our nature is to want to help everyone rather than define a niche group of people we can help. We just don't want anyone left out!)

Find Your Prospects

Your ideal client is someone that needs what you have to offer and is willing to pay for it. I was certain that my ideal client was the producer on the street—the ones that actually do the selling in the field or over the phone. But I was dead wrong. That was my end user, not my client! My clients were Sales Managers, Sales Leaders, Vice Presidents of Sales, and HR Directors. They may or may not use my training in their own jobs, but they needed my services to help their sales force generate more revenue. Moreover, they could pay for it. So, before you jump to conclusions about your ideal client, take a few minutes to dig deeper and get really clear on whom you're targeting.

Here are some questions to ask yourself:

- What are the key characteristics of your ideal client?

- If you could describe them in a brief sentence, what would that be?

- Does the client you have in mind have the ability to write a check or authorize payment, or is someone above them the ultimate decision-maker?

- What does your client need? Make sure it's in their words and not yours.

- What do they want? Wants are different than needs; for example, a client may want to work with someone locally to provide a solution for their need.

- Where do your clients hang out? Where can you find them, both online and offline?

When you have that clear picture of who they are, your job is now to connect with them. To accomplish this, you need to set goals for yourself, and systematize how you will build and manage your business.

Are you focused on the target? You should be able to describe your ideal client in 30 seconds.

Study the Masters

Do you know what it takes to be great in your field? If not, find out. Study the most successful people in your industry. What sets them apart? Is it their message? Their marketing? Look at the tools they are using to promote themselves and their product or services. What information is available on their website? Are they active in social media? Do they make regular television and radio appearances, offer consulting services, or speak in front of different groups? By studying the masters, you can create your own roadmap to success simply by walking in their footsteps.

The following worksheet can help you quantify the traits that foster success in your industry and help you establish goals for your own business. In the left column, write down the name of a successful person or business that you want to emulate. In the right column, write down the traits you believe have helped set that leader apart, including how they market their products or services.

SUCCESS TRAITS WORKSHEET

Industry Leader or Role Model	Success Traits

Once you have discovered what it takes to achieve greatness, formulate your goals accordingly. A simple goal can help you stay focused and keep you from quitting. (In the first year or two of your business, odds are you'll think about throwing in the towel more than a few times. Just remember, it's a marathon, not a sprint. Persistence pays off!)

Set the Pace

Losing focus is easy when you are launching a start-up, even if it's a one-person operation, because you inevitably have to wear many different hats. One day, you are the CEO, the next you're VP of Marketing, and the next you're head of the Accounting Department. With so many tasks on your To Do List, it can be easy to shuffle things around to suit your mood rather than your timeline. We are all guilty of procrastinating and being distracted by shiny objects—especially when working from home—and for many the busiest day of the year is "tomorrow."

Setting goals gives you short-term motivation and long-term vision. By knowing what results you want to achieve, you can better organize your time and resources, and you can experience the pride of accomplishment as you hit your milestones along the way. Achieving even minor goals can provide continuous motivation and boost your self-confidence, keeping you on track, focused and interested as you get your business off the ground.

You will want to set short-term, medium-term and long-term goals. Make sure the short-terms goals build toward the medium-term goals and that the medium-term goals put you on track to accomplish the long-term goals. Once you've done this, make an agreement with yourself regarding what "price" you are willing to pay to reach your goals. Will you have to take out a loan? Put in 12-hour workdays? Forgo vacation for the first two years? Whatever sacrifices you will have to make, commit to them in writing. Make a contract with yourself to achieve your goals—each one outlined clearly with a timeframe and deliverables. Then, to quote a famous shoe company, "Just Do It."

Here are some ways to help make sure you hit your goals continuously:

1. **Know your objective.** Document exactly what it is that you want and need to achieve. Be precise.

2. **Set up action steps.** How will you get there? What is your timeframe? Do you need help? Chunk larger goals into smaller tasks, so you can make forward progress every day.

3. **Keep score.** Establish checkpoints or milestones along the way, so you can quickly determine whether you are still on track or need to make adjustments to correct your course.

4. **Be accountable.** Schedule a weekly coffee date with a business coach, mentor, or fellow entrepreneur to check in on your status. Having someone else hold you accountable can help you keep your eye on the prize.

5. **Reward yourself.** Nothing feels better than reaching your goals and receiving a small token of appreciation—even if it's from yourself!

Taking time to set goals that are realistically achievable within a given time frame is critical to your success as an entrepreneur, because your short- and long-term goals help define the destination. Clearly stated goals also give you a route to follow and help you to stay focused, gain more confidence, track your progress, and celebrate your achievements.

Stick With It

Regrettably, simply setting goals is not enough to ensure your success in business—you have to actually do the actions necessary to achieve your goals. For this reason, goal-setting without self-belief and discipline is simply a waste of time. As an entrepreneur, you may have a blueprint of what you want to achieve in your business, but without the necessary discipline to carry out the plan, you won't achieve the desired results.

Remember, too, that goal-setting in business is never complete without a timeframe within which the goal will be achieved. A timeframe will help you determine whether you need to fast-track a certain task or slow down a bit to keep the horse and cart in proper order. Again, having short-, medium- and long-term goals can provide a strong framework for building your business, and provide continuous motivation along the way.

In the next chapter, we'll explore the fundamental resources and strategies that will help you get your

business off the ground. You will need to establish goals
and timeframes to put each of these into place—which
means investing the time and energy to put your roadmap
on paper.

All that writing down of plans and targets can be
frustrating when all you want is to run your business.
But, the more clearly you document your goals and
milestones from the outset, the easier it will be to stay on
track during the start-up phase of your new venture. You
will also be creating a solid framework and developing
excellent habits for long-term success. As a bonus, you
get to experience happy bursts of increased self-esteem
as you routinely accomplish goals that you have set for
yourself and your business.

CHAPTER THREE

LAY THE FOUNDATION

When I started my business, I was simply going to be a trainer. A trainer in sales, to be exact. I had so much fun and received so many great testimonials from people I had trained throughout my sales career that I wanted to continue in that path and just add the gender communications piece. That would be my niche. I had it all worked out.

Then I thought about the dip in the economy and figured I probably needed to make some adjustments. Okay, so maybe I wouldn't be a trainer. Maybe I would be a consultant, or a professional networker. No wait, an author. Nope, a speaker. The more I tried to pursue my passion, the more my head was spinning. I wasn't focused, because everything sounded great and yet nothing sounded great. I was already out there telling people about my new venture, and everyone thought I was wildly successful. I never shared what kept me up at night. That wasn't my style. I was practicing "fake it till you make it" entrepreneurship—the most stressful way to start a new business.

I had enough money socked away to be comfortable for a while, but that 'while' was getting closer and closer. I would get a retainer with a company for six months or so, and instead of lining up more clients in case the retainer ended, I let my pipeline dry up. Isn't the first rule of sales to keep your pipeline full? Back when I was in sales and would take a few weeks off, I would have business to turn in before I left and business to turn in when I got back. My pipeline was full. So what happened? It worked then so why not now?

Build Your Systems

Working in sales, I had a system for everything. I had a set routine for making follow-up calls to prospects and reaching out to referrals. I would send birthday cards to clients and drop a thank-you note in the mail after every meeting. Even though my efforts were focused on building and nurturing relationships, in effect, I was marketing. My pipeline back then came from referrals. Since I was now embarking on a new business, I would have to fill my new pipeline with leads from a variety of sources. And that would require a marketing plan.

Track prospects until they either become a client or they don't. Develop a long-term drip campaign for those that don't—they might just provide a referral in the future.

The vast majority of my clients have come through

networking and referrals, which have led to speaking engagements and retainer contracts for my consulting services. Regardless of your industry, you will need to determine the best strategy for generating new business, and put in place a clearly defined process for following up on leads and converting them to customers. Here are just a few questions to consider:

1. **How will people find you?** Consider the foundation of your marketing strategy, whether it is search engine optimization, pay-per-click advertising, speaking engagements, or networking meetings. Knowing where your potential clients congregate, both online and offline, will help define your approach.

2. **How will they connect with you?** You need systems and processes in place to get peoples' information, so that you can establish regular communication. Will you have lead capture forms on your website? Run special promotions? Distribute a survey when you speak at events? When someone hands you a business card, do you have a process in place for getting it into your CRM system (or at least your Microsoft Outlook contact list) and scheduling a follow-up call or face-to-face meeting?

3. **How will you convert leads to customers?** Unless you have a clearly defined sales process in place—from first contact through contract

in hand—odds are, valuable prospects will fall through the cracks. Take the time to map out your system in detail, including the number and timing of follow-up calls and emails, as well as forms that you need, such as contracts and non-disclosure agreements. Consider any special incentives that you will make available to close a sale, as well as nurture campaigns for prospects who are not ready to take action immediately. Each step should be meticulously scripted—both the text and the timing—so there is no variance in your process.

Pick Your Dream Team

As an entrepreneur, you will inevitably wear many hats, but that does not mean you need to wear *every* hat. When I first launched my business, I knew that social media would play an important role in my promotional strategy. Am I a social media expert? Far from it! Facebook, LinkedIn and Twitter didn't exist when I was working full-time in sales, and although I understood the value of participating in these types of social networks, I had no idea how to formulate a social strategy for my business. Similarly, I knew that having a website was paramount, but I had neither the time nor the technical savvy to put one together myself.

Start assembling your Dream Team from the beginning to get your business off the ground. You can always add more members later.

My Dream Team started with my son, PJ, who just so happens to be a Web developer. He was able to build a site for me in short order, and at a price I could afford. Of course, not everyone has a close family member with this skill set. Take your time when looking for the right person or company to build your website. You will be embarking on a long-term relationship with your Webmaster, because you will need to continually update your site as your business grows. You want someone whom you not only trust, but who understands and cares about your business. I also recommend that you consider building your website on a flexible content management system, like WordPress, rather than in straight HTML. This type of structure will make it much easier for you to add and edit content on your site at minimal expense. (I picked up this little tip later in my entrepreneurial journey from another expert on my Dream Team.)

My next team member was Jason Markow, whom PJ had met on a trip to Austin, Texas, for the South by Southwest Conference. Although PJ was able to build my website, he is not a Web designer. Jason is, and the introduction was made. We scheduled a call to get to know each

DREAM TEAM PLAYERS

Depending on your business, you may need to add some or all of these players to your Dream Team:
- Web Developer
- Social Media Manager
- Business Coach
- CPA
- Attorney
- Manufacturer
- Distribution Broker
- Administrative Asst.
- Printer

other and essentially conduct a mutual interview, to see whether we would be a good fit. The call went well, but I was painfully naïve and didn't know what I really needed. Jason, light years ahead of his chronological age, was very patient. At one point he asked me whether I had any other questions, and I calmly responded that I didn't even know the questions to ask. I did tell him that he needed to treat me like his mom and not make me cry. He assured me that would be no problem. (In the past three years, he has only made me cry once—by accident—so I would say we are doing great.)

Jason picked up where PJ left off, taking my site to a new level of functionality and visual polish. He is also an Internet strategist and has helped me immensely in codifying my approach to online marketing, particularly through social media, a topic we will explore later in more detail.

In addition to PJ and Jason, I have a supporting cast of characters who are available to offer help and guidance, as I need them. Many of these professionals have become dear friends and have nearly as much invested emotionally in my business as I do. Although each entrepreneurial venture may require different players on the Dream Team, it's a safe bet that you will need an attorney and a CPA, as well as a marketing consultant and a business coach. If you are producing a physical product, you may need to connect with a manufacturing consultant or distribution broker. I encourage you to speak with other entrepreneurs in your industry to find out what other roles may be necessary to make your personal Dream Team complete.

Establish Your Brand

Once you have your team in place, you are ready for launch! As the first order of business, you need to make people aware of your presence. That means it's time to get busy putting your promotional materials together. I highly recommend that you not go about this the way I did when I first launched my business.

As I mentioned, I had already established numerous connections through networking, a marketing strategy that comes very naturally to me, because I am a people person. After deciding that I would promote myself as a sales trainer specializing in gender communications, I floated the concept of "Selling in a Skirt" by several dozen participants at local business networking meetings. The reaction was extremely positive.

Create your irresistible brand, then become it.

I conducted this informal research for about a month, asking people about their challenges when it came to sales, and each time I was getting the confirmation that focusing on gender communication issues was a great idea. But, at this point, all I had was a name and a business card—that was it. No website, no brochures, and no Dream Team. Just a great idea and a lot of chutzpah!

I was at a pretty big Chamber of Commerce meeting when a woman introduced herself to me and asked what I was so excited about, since she had seen me looking very animated while I was speaking with other guests at the event. I presented her with my elevator pitch and she told me that I was exactly who she was looking for to speak at her next meeting. The conversation that followed was both thrilling and awkward.

Woman: Do you have a website?

Me: It's being updated and should be ready soon.

Woman: Are you speaking any place locally, so I can hear you?

Me: I'll be in Knoxville, Tennessee this weekend. (I had not been hired to speak anywhere, but I was going to visit a friend, so I was stating a fact.)

Woman: Honey, that's not close to Dallas. Do you have a brochure?

Me: Did you want one emailed to you or mailed?

Woman: Mailed. I would like a physical copy to review.

Me: Perfect! I will get one right out to you. (A mailed copy would give me a few extra days to get my act together.)

You see, despite my rampant enthusiasm about

becoming an entrepreneur, I wasn't prepared for anyone to really ask me to do business. I had a name and a business card. So what did I do? What every normal, hardworking businesswoman would do—I called my son and started to cry.

PJ managed to talk me off the ledge, and he reminded me that I should be ecstatic over the fact that someone asked me to speak at their event. He quickly got to work putting together a website and a brochure in a matter of days, and life was good again. I had my programs set and a website that worked and looked good and a brochure that spelled it all out. In an effort to spare you the same drama and help you get a head start on your business success, here is a checklist of the promotional tools and resources you should have in place when you launch your new venture.

MARKETING CHECKLIST

Business Cards – This is the most simple, cost-effective method of self-promotion. Never leave home without them. Hand your business card to people you meet, and make sure they know what you do and that you're available should they need what you offer. Keep additional cards in your car and your wallet, so you will never be caught off guard. (You would be surprised how many people come to networking events and forget their business cards!)

Website – Your website should illustrate exactly what you do and have a clear call to action for visitors. Many entrepreneurs leave out the second part, crafting a website that talks all about their product or services, without inviting visitors to contact them for help. Remember, people coming to your website have a need. You must identify and address that need, explain how you provide a solution, and motivate them to get in touch.

Case in point: I saw a website for a plumber that featured a picture of the plumber standing in front of his new truck, another one of him next to a fleet of trucks, and one of him in front of his new house. Nowhere on the homepage did I see a photo of him fixing a leaky faucet or draining water out of a basement. Wouldn't those be problems that would cause you to call him? Remember who your audience is and make sure your website speaks to their needs!

SEO – In addition to building your website, you need to make sure that it is picked up by search engines, so that people looking online for what you have can find you. Not every website designer knows about search engine optimization (SEO), and you may need to add another player to your Dream Team to address this part of your marketing strategy.

Video – Posting online videos can be very effective for establishing your brand, engendering trust, and improving your SEO. People want to buy from people they know, and if they watch you on a video, they feel like they know you. Of course, make sure that your video is professional. That doesn't mean you have to spend thousands of dollars, but it does mean that you should look pulled together. If you can't afford to work with a production house, you can record videos in your office or at home—just make sure you don't have wrinkled clothes, a messy desk, kids poking their heads in during taping or the dog barking in the background. You also want to have good lighting on your face and use a high definition (HD) camera or webcam. Professional is the order of the day!

Social Media – Connect with like-minded people and find your fans through Facebook, Twitter, Google Plus, LinkedIn and a handful of other sites for social networking. You will be surprised how people will start to follow you if you have interesting and valuable information to share. Your goal is not to have millions of people "like" you or follow you. Your goal is to find the right people to do that and then start a conversation with them. Comment on their posts and tweets. When they respond, continue the dialog. You will be amazed that you can cultivate a relationship with people all over the world. They will start sharing your posts and tweets and blogs, and sooner rather than later, you will all be sharing information.

As with all marketing, consistency is key. I post an encouraging message to Facebook, LinkedIn and Twitter every morning. People frequently stop me at networking meetings and speaking engagements to tell me that they look for my posts to help them through the day. What a great way to stay top-of-mind! With that said, if you don't have the time to manage your social media accounts regularly, plenty of people you can hire are available to do it for you. Just make sure they truly understand your brand and your voice, and set clear boundaries from the start about how they should initiate conversations and respond to others' messages.

Blog Posts – Adding relevant, informative content to your website regularly can give visitors a reason to keep coming back. Search engines like to see fresh content, as well, which can improve your site's ranking. A blog post is really a story told in about 500 words. The tone can be informal, even conversational, as long as the content is on point. Your goal is to share valuable information and to do so consistently, so you build up your community (which means you are building relationships). Your blog is a great forum for answering common questions, educating readers, and highlighting successful case studies. Again, shine the light on your customer.

Newsletters – Build up a list of friends, family and fans and, with their permission, send out a quarterly or monthly e-newsletter with updates about what you're working on. Be sure to add useful content that can benefit the reader, like quick tips or something educational. Although you may want to include special offers and announcements about your latest accomplishments, your e-newsletter should not be purely self-promotional. Also, make sure the layout is not so busy that people hit the Delete button before they read the content. And, of course, be sure to include an obvious place to sign up for the e-newsletter on your website.

Brochures – Some people will say that having a print brochure in this day and age is a waste of money, since so much communication happens electronically. I disagree. With the power of print-on-demand, you no longer need to print 10,000 copies of your brochure to get a decent price; rather, you can do short runs for a small investment and have collateral available when you need it. I use my brochure when I am meeting someone for a 1:1 appointment, when I send out my media kit, and when I am a vendor at a trade show. With print on demand, you can also change your message or images or add something new. This lets you have an additional touch point with your clients, because you can send out an updated brochure to announce a new program or service.

Press Releases – Learn how to send press releases to the media when you have something to announce. Maybe you just became president of an association, or you were asked to be on a board, or you just wrote a book. When sent at the right time and to the right people, press releases can help generate extra publicity. When you're just starting out, you don't need to hire an expensive PR firm. You can use online wire services, like eReleases.com or PRWeb, and make follow-up calls to local reporters yourself.

Networking – Get out of your office and meet people in person! Go to trade shows, networking events and charity fundraisers. Remember that people do business with people they know and trust. Meeting folks in person will help with that. We'll explore networking strategies in more detail in a later chapter.

Stay On It

Of course, don't think for a moment that once you have your website, marketing materials, programs or anything else in place that it will be your final plan. Marketing is always a work in progress, both as your business grows and as the marketplace changes. Embrace updates! You can't have a personal connection with materials or a large ego when you are an entrepreneur. Things change faster than you can imagine.

Also, you need to market yourself consistently. Whether it's a blog post, a newsletter, a tweet or whatever, you need to include some sort of marketing activity in your daily routine. Not everyone will be looking for your product or service every day. If you market once in a while, it may not be at the time someone is looking for you. If you do it routinely, your name and information will be in front of your target audience on a regular basis. When they need you, you will be there.

In the next chapter, we'll delve a little deeper into marketing and explore a strategy that can really set you apart from the competition. As the song from the Broadway musical Gypsy goes, "You've gotta get a gimmick, if you wanna get ahead!"

CHAPTER FOUR

CARVE YOUR NICHE

When you think about defining your ideal client, what you are really trying to do is identify your niche market. For example, your product or service may target adult women who have children at home. But, when you drill down deeper, your true niche may be single working mothers in their 30s and 40s with children between the ages of newborn and six years old. This sub-set of the broader working-mom-market has very specific needs, because there is not another parent at home to care for their children, and the children are not yet in school.

Knowing your niche is important, because it will not only help you better define the features and pricing for your product or service, it will let you tailor your marketing message to address the needs and wants of a specific and narrow group. Marketing experts say that the narrower the niche, the stronger your business will be, as long as you choose a niche that is accurate and reflects an authentic need.

Here are just a few reasons why defining your niche market can benefit your bottom line:

1. **Market subsets are more profitable.** A smaller group has very specific and unique needs and wants, allowing you to charge a premium for the customized solutions you offer.

2. **You will get more referrals.** When people know exactly what your specialty is, they also know exactly whom to send your way. Referrals are the most expensive free lead you can receive—they don't cost anything, but they have tremendous value. Ultimately they should become the bread-and-butter of your business.

3. **You can find business allies.** Working within a narrow market provides a great opportunity to partner with complementary businesses that serve the same market. Knowing your niche will help you zero in on who would and would not be a great strategic partner.

4. **You will be laser focused on your target.** Defining your niche takes a lot of the guesswork out of your marketing efforts, and also positions you as a clear expert in your area.

Narrow Your Focus

One of the most common mistakes that entrepreneurs make when they decide to hone in on a niche market is changing their mind. Often, they fear that they will lose business to competitors outside of their niche, so they opt for a broad-market approach. They try to sell to everyone, and as we determined early on, "everyone" is not a market, unless you are selling air.

Here are a few tips to help you feel more confident about niche marketing for your business:

Be selective. You can't be all things to all people. You have to identify who your ideal customers are and say no to everyone else. If we look at the last election, a number of niche demographics were important to some candidates and not to others. The way the candidates targeted those populations—including college students, women, minorities, and teachers, among other groups—definitely helped sway the outcome.

Remember, it's not about you. Marketing is about telling prospective clients how you can meet their needs, and the more focused you are, the better. What are you providing that is new and compelling? If your product or service is not that specialized, how can you tailor it to accommodate a specific niche?

Always test-market. Market research is like sticking your toe into a lake before jumping in. If you figure out exactly which group of people you want to reach, and what their needs are, you avoid wasting time and money. Once you know, you can alter your product or services to fit the needs of your target market more closely, and you can create a message that reflects your business and your customer.

Know your direct competitors. How will you stack up against them? What are they doing that you like and, more importantly, that you don't like? If there is no existing competition, that may not be a good sign. Although it might indicate that other companies haven't found a way to provide a product or service that your niche will want to buy, it could also mean that others have tried and failed to appeal to the specific group you are targeting.

Defining a niche market will keep you more focused and can bring more referrals.

Draw the Bulls Eye

I am often asked about my niche market and how I chose it. A fundamental rule of entrepreneurship is to do what you know. In my case, I lived the life of my niche. I was a woman in a male-dominated field throughout my entire career, even as I changed industries. So, when I walked away from my last position, I asked myself what I would have benefited from during my years in the field. What would have made my life easier, and how can I do that for someone else?

I knew what it was like to be the only female or to be one of very few females on a large sales team. That was my "a-ha" moment. If I'd had just one female mentor or coach, or a woman who extended her hand to offer me guidance, suggestions or friendship in the workplace, my entire professional journey would have been markedly easier.

As you think about identifying your niche market, describe who or what it is in great detail. Think very specifically about whom you want to work with and how your experience can help them achieve their goals. Here are a few factors to consider:

- Will you be serving women or men?

- Does it matter whether they are married or have children?

- What age group are you targeting? Young adults? Seniors?

- Will what you offer apply to one specific industry?

- What income level are your clients?

- Are they high school graduates? College educated? MBAs?

- Are they tech-savvy? Do they use social media?

Depending on the type of business you are launching, your list of questions may be much longer and include factors like how your clients commute to work or what type of car they drive, whether they live in the city or the suburbs, whether they have any specific health issues, or whether they own their own home. The possibilities are endless, but until you know who your market is, what they look like, where they hang out and what they need, you don't have your niche.

Just like with your business plan, you can increase your chances of success when you put these thoughts and strategies on paper. Writing down the details about your ideal client will also help keep you fixed on the right target in your marketing and networking efforts and provide a valuable roadmap to keep you on course as your business grows.

Keep Your Focus

I have a tendency to be distracted by shiny objects—or, to be more accurate, shiny business opportunities. As an entrepreneur, staying focused is critical. My gut always tells me when I have gone astray. You know the feeling you get when you go against your instincts? If I agree to do something that may not be part of my true niche, my stomach reacts—a clear signal that I am not focused on my primary target.

To ensure that I don't succumb to that type of temptation in the future, my business coach led me through a strategy session in which we defined what I was "allowed" to do in my business. It's called my Strategic Triangle. A triangle has three angles, and the rule is that anything I do in my business has to fit into one of those angles. My triangle is speaking, coaching and training. If an opportunity comes along that doesn't fit into one of those categories, I cannot do it. If I want to add something to my triangle, I have to eliminate something else. See how it works? I will explain the process through which I defined my Strategic Triangle in a later chapter.

It took time for me to learn to trust my gut, and early in my entrepreneurial career, I made my share of mistakes.

THE STRATEGIC TRIANGLE IN ACTION

A close friend of mine recently applied the Strategic Triangle in her business, a marketing agency that she owns with her husband. The company offers website design, mobile application development, and video production services. Often, clients will come to them with a related need, such as graphic design for a print brochure or SEO consulting for a website. My friend would take on those projects, because she was hesitant to turn down a check. Eventually, she realized that the team was reinventing the wheel every time they tried to deliver something that fell outside the three core components of the business.

Did the company have the talent and resources to do special projects? Absolutely. But, the time spent creating a new system for a short assignment ate into the profitability and caused a breakdown in the existing systems they had in place for Web, video and mobile, often causing other projects to be late. Now, she will turn down special projects that fall outside of the company's Strategic Triangle, and the business is more profitable as a result.

For example, one time I was offered a contract from a high profile company to do their sales training. I was flattered to have been asked, and the money was great, so I said yes. When I got home after the meeting, my stomach was doing somersaults. My head said yes, but my gut wanted to know, "Are you crazy?"

Not only would I have to build and deliver the training, but the program this client needed had nothing to do with Selling in a Skirt. In my head, I continued to try and justify my decision by focusing on the income, but my stomach was winning the internal struggle. In the end,

I called and declined the offer. Guess what? My stomach was fine, so I knew I had made the right decision.

Press the Flesh

Once you have clearly defined your niche market, you need to get the word out. Personally, I am passionate about building relationships. I love connecting people and businesses, and I love connecting with people period. So, when I started my sales training business, I thought if I just connected with a few contacts and each of them told two people and then they told two people, I would have a flood of clients in no time.

Getting things off the ground wasn't quite that easy, of course. But networking with people face-to-face was a huge factor in my early success and continues to benefit my business today. We'll explore networking more in the next chapter. For now, consider how you can best connect with your target clients in person. Where do they hang out? Who do they know? Tailor your work schedule so you can be where the prospects are as often as possible.

Attract Followers

Social media is especially effective when you are working within a niche market, because you already know so much about your audience and can connect with them on a more personal level. I am somewhat technologically challenged, so Jason from my Dream Team helped me first get familiar with the different social networks and how to navigate them. He walked me through each site and explained why the business should or should not have a presence there.

Personally, I focus my efforts on LinkedIn, Twitter and Facebook. I have a different reason and strategy for using each network. I also subscribe to HARO (Help a Reporter Out), PitchRate and Reporter Connection, because these sites look for experts in various niches and I consider myself an expert in my field—as should anyone who has narrowed down their specific market segment to the same degree.

Make Adjustments

Add the speed and volume of social media to the relationships you build meeting people through networking events and conferences, and you will hit a home run in your niche marketing efforts. But what happens when what you thought was your niche market changes, or needs to change? I believe you constantly have to continue your market research and see how your market niche or the needs of your target clients may have evolved.

For instance, when I started as a consultant, I was strictly working with women. I figured, I am a woman, I know what women need, and I know what I needed—case closed. But, more than one man, dozens in fact, asked me why I closed my niche to men. The answer seemed obvious to me, but in the interest of fairness, I conducted an informal survey to find out the biggest challenge for men in sales management. Know what they said? They were trying desperately to bring women into their field, but didn't know where to find them. And, when they found them, they didn't know how to recruit them, train them, motivate and retain them.

With this new information in mind, I adjusted my niche market to include both men and women. This may seem like a significant broadening of my niche, but I made several more adjustments to narrow down the focus again.

For one thing, I looked at new statistical data about women and learned that more wealth passes through women's hands than men, that Baby Boomer women would be coming into a double windfall over the next 15 years as their parents and husbands passed away, and that 85 percent of all consumer purchases are made by women. The puzzle pieces were falling into place. My niche didn't depend on whether the clients I was serving were male or female—my focus needed to be on teaching them how to communicate with women effectively. Whether you are a man or a woman, understanding how women think and make decisions is vital for success in sales. I redefined my niche to focus on gender communications in sales training. So, yes, I did start to color outside the original box, but I stayed on the same page.

Be Authoritative

Having a niche market can help position you as an expert in your field, because the field itself is very small. As an expert, you have the authority to speak about your subject matter with conviction and show that you mean business. You can also differentiate yourself from the competition by focusing on your narrow market segment.

I am often asked whether you need a book to be

considered an expert. Let's put it this way: although you don't have to have a book to be considered an expert, you are considered an expert when you have a book. Here's the deal, though—some people write a book and want to be a #1 best-selling author. That was not my goal. I wrote a book for two reasons. The first was to get 30 years of stories, experiences and lessons organized in a way that made sense to others and could benefit them in their own careers. The second was to use it as a calling card and give books to those people I wanted to hear my message, if they couldn't hear it directly from me. My first book, *Selling in a Skirt,* is a business book, but it has tips that you can implement right away to increase sales. Also, even though men might be inclined to dismiss the book based on its title, *Selling in a Skirt,* the tagline is, *The Secrets Women Don't Know They Know About Sales (And What Men Should Know, Too).* So, I have my entire niche covered.

Tweak, But Don't Stray

Through the years, I had to adjust my niche a bit, but my message never changed. My message has always been about communication. How women communicate, how men communicate and how everyone communicates with each other. I never say one gender is better than the other or one is right and one is wrong; I talk about the differences between men and women, and how to use them as assets rather than liabilities. Although I may be speaking to different industries, my message remains solid.

In the next chapter, we'll explore a very different approach to marketing—one that I have found to be the most effective and enduring way to win new clients. Although technology makes it easier to reach more people faster at a fraction of what it used to cost, the most powerful connections still happen face-to-face.

CHAPTER FIVE

EXPAND YOUR NETWORK

Since I am a sales trainer and teach the entire sales process, sometimes, "Do what I say, not what I do" is my mantra. But, when I was building this business, I had to practice what I preached when it came to networking and prospecting.

I have been in sales for 30 years, with more than 15 years in the insurance industry. I was a Producer, a Sales Leader, and then an Agency Manager. I trained and recruited for many years and showed others how to prospect and not rely on leads. During my stint in Corporate America as a Sales Director, I was asked to move to Dallas to help build a training department. A couple of years in, I decided that this was not a position I wanted to keep, so I resigned and started my business. Taking the plunge into entrepreneurship is already stressful, but in my case, the level of anxiety was amped up significantly. You see, when I moved to Dallas, I moved by myself.

My children were grown, and so I was no longer seeking out other parents or people involved in kids' activities with whom I needed to connect. What's more, when I was working in my corporate position, I was on a plane most of the time, and when I was home I was in the office or catching up with my life. I did not have an active network, either personally or professionally, and I was in a new city. When I started this business, I did not know one person in the Dallas area. How can you start a business with no contacts? It's like trying to build a business online without a list. It can be done, but it will be an uphill battle—a scenario I am quite used to but was hoping was behind me.

Go Out on a Limb
Let's just say that I had to step way out of my comfort zone to get my new consulting venture off the ground. I spent six solid months networking and making connections. Now, people refer to me as the networking queen and talk about the fact that I seem to know everyone wherever I go. Little do they know the work it took to get there.

Why is networking such a critical strategy for business growth? Consider these factors:

- Anyone can do it.

- No classes or formal training are necessary.

- People do business with people they know and trust.

- It can be extremely affordable.

- You can serve as a resource to help others succeed.

- You can market yourself and your business in a relaxed, social situation.

Whenever I coach anyone and we talk about networking, they always want the shortcut. Many people are almost as afraid of networking as they are of public speaking. Although there is no real shortcut to successful networking, the following guidelines can help you get the most from your efforts, whether you are a pro or a newbie to the networking game:

> **Arrive early.** The thing I hated the most about networking (or any event, for that matter) was walking into a room and imagining that everyone was staring at me. I was way off base in my thinking—something I will get to later in this chapter—but getting there first helped me cope with my anxieties. By arriving early, you can avoid the experience of walking into a room of strangers. Instead, you will already be there and people will walk up to you to begin a conversation. In addition, you will have the best opportunity to meet everyone, since you have a little extra time for networking.

> **Arrive with a goal in mind.** Before the meeting, set a goal for yourself for that day, and then achieve it. Many times people go to a networking event with the intent of collecting business cards. What will you do with that pile on your desk? My goal for every event was to meet three amazing people with whom I could start a relationship. When I came across someone

I found interesting, I would make a point to let them know they were one of the three. Sharing this tidbit definitely started a great conversation.

Bring a pen. After someone gives you their business card, jot down on the back of the card where you met them or any information that might be useful when you follow up with them later. Another helpful trick is to fold down a corner of the business card for someone that you would like to get to know better. That way, if you have a whole collection of cards at the end of an event, the one or two with bent corners will stand out from the pack (and the notes on the back of each will jog your memory). Of course, be sure to bring plenty of business cards with you to networking events, too!

Mix and mingle. Don't huddle up with co-workers or friends. You are less likely to be approached by others if you appear to be busy with idle conversation. Likewise, don't be afraid to approach people you don't know and introduce yourself. After all, that's what networking is all about. Do your best to remember names of individuals as soon as you first meet them, and ask plenty of questions about their business. Don't hard sell yourself or your company. Networking meetings are to be social and more relaxed than formal business events, like conferences and workshops.

Those tips cover the fundamentals, but as I mentioned, I took networking to an entirely different level.

Invest Your Time

I have been told that I have done more networking in 60 days than others have done in six months or even six years. How else do you get yourself out there? Success in any line of work is based as much on whom you know as what you know. You have to get some skin in the game to make those connections, even if it means stepping far outside of your comfort zone.

With that in mind, here are some additional pointers to get the most return on your investment in networking:

- Explore many different groups and events, so you can explore the group dynamics and determine which meetings are the best fit.

- Dress professionally. This is not a day at the beach or a night at the club. A polished outfit will ensure that you are taken seriously. (As a woman, this is especially important. When in doubt, choose a more conservative look over the latest fashion trend.)

- Smile! People are more inclined to approach someone who appears happy and confident.

- Shake hands with everyone you meet. Sometimes a firm handshake breaks the ice.

- Be prepared with your 30-second explanation of how you solve problems through the product or service you provide.

- When sharing about your business with others, ask about theirs.

- Sincerely listen to what others are saying. Ask follow-up questions to learn as much as you can about the people you meet.

- When appropriate, introduce others in your Circle of Influence to those you have met when you feel there could be a mutually beneficial relationship.

- Follow up on all referrals you are given. They are a gift to you! Make sure you treat each referral the way you would want to be treated.

- Build relationships. Learn how to ask questions and listen to what the other person needs so that you can help to make things happen.

Of course, in addition to mastering the positive aspects of networking, you also want to avoid faux pas and bad habits as you seek to establish valuable business connections. Here is my Top Ten List of things I have learned *not* to do in networking:

1. **Don't make networking your full-time job.** You can get very busy attending networking events every day, but you cannot build your business if your attention is on your meeting calendar rather than your core operations.

2. **Decide which groups will benefit you most and join up.** It is worth the investment in your business to pay membership dues to the groups

you found most interesting and useful. That said, you can go broke if you join every one, so don't over commit yourself.

3. **Nix the "what's in it for me" attitude.** Networking is all about building relationships. If you approach each connection as a potential cash cow for your business, you will certainly stand out in the crowd, but for the wrong reason.

4. **Don't surround yourself with people you already know.** That is called "hanging out," not networking.

5. **Don't obsess over everyone's opinion.** You will know when you are networking too much, because opinions will start be contradictory and it can bring you to tears. When you hit 'opinion overload,' it's a sign that you need to be more selective about the time you invest in meetings.

6. **Don't second-guess yourself.** Yes, you want to get input from other professionals, but no one knows your business the way you do. Everyone has an opinion about what works for them. Some are very successful and some are just faking it until they make it. If you believe in what you are doing, stick with it.

7. **Schedule 1:1 meetings selectively.** You might feel super popular when you look at your calendar and every breakfast, lunch, dinner and

coffee break is booked for the next two weeks. But if you sit down with every person you meet, you'll be taking precious time away from your business. Schedule meetings with a purpose that is beneficial to both parties.

8. **Don't take things personally.** Occasionally, a group may not be right for you, or you're simply not right for the group. Some groups will invite you to attend as a guest and then may or may not extend an invitation to join. Things happen the way they are supposed to, and if you don't see a welcome mat at your feet, it means you should keep on walking.

9. **Don't make everyone your friend.** Remember women develop and cultivate relationships. In this case, however, you are looking for business connections, not buddies. Be careful you don't cross the line and make everyone your new best friend. The point of networking is to build your business and help others do the same.

10. **Avoid talking politics and religion.** Networking is just like dating. You are having your first date and trying to make a good enough impression to get a second one. The bottom line is, you don't want to alienate anyone who may be a prospective client.

At its very core, networking is based on a simple principle we were all taught when we were young, which holds true no matter how old you are: People do business with those they like and trust. So, while you are out making new contacts, be sure that your focus is on the person with whom you are speaking and not on you. Remember, people do business with people...not businesses!

Although I once greatly disliked networking, today I am a master connector. In many ways, I simple learned to change my perspective. Remember my fear of walking into a room full of strangers? I likened the experience to having dinner in a restaurant alone and reading a book. In my mind, I was convinced that everyone must be thinking, "That's so sad, she has to eat alone," when in reality others might be envious of having quiet time to catch up on some reading. It's all about perception, and when it came to networking, my radar was way off. People attend networking events because they want to meet new people. Walking into a room full of strangers is a good thing, because it's like walking into a room filled with fresh opportunities and exciting new relationships.

Today, my mental Rolodex® goes into overdrive when I attend a networking event. I make it my goal to help others make connections, and just by listening to people I can usually come up with 8-10 great recommendations. My process of connecting is simple:

- I meet someone.

- We have a 1:1 meeting and get to know each other; the relationship begins.

- From that meeting, I come up with a list of potential

prospects.

- I introduce the two parties via email with a description of who they are, what they do, and why I believe they should know each other.

- I invite them to connect.

That's it, plain and simple. I am proud to say that I have helped foster dozens of powerful connections between friends and associates.

Networking is one of the easiest, most cost effective, and most fruitful means of growing your business as an entrepreneur.

Draw the Line

My ability to connect others has paid off in my own business countless times, but I will admit that the effort is not always reciprocated. Either the person with whom I'm meeting can't think of anyone they believe I should meet, or they have a list of possible connections for me and never follow through. Even with some gentle nudging, the introductions never come. Although I go into each 1:1 meeting with no expectations and will gladly let someone buy me lunch or dinner to "pick my brains," sometimes, the favor has to be returned. If you find that you are putting more time into helping others reach their goals than you are working on your own business, you may need to set a boundary to limit the amount of time and effort you are willing to invest.

Focus Your Efforts

The purpose of networking is to find prospects, plain and simple. Yes, you want to help other business people make connections and act as a sounding board for their ideas. In the end, however, you want to drive clients to your door. In the early days of my networking efforts, I overlooked this objective.

The first time I went to a networking event, I walked into the room and froze. I literally froze in my tracks. I didn't want to walk around and introduce myself to complete strangers, but I knew I needed to if I were to ever get my sales training business off the ground. So, I found the loneliest person in the room and sat down with him at a table. Neither of us spoke, but heck, I was networking. At least I was there in the room!

After repeating that feeble approach a few times, I realized it was pure craziness and decided to actually speak to a few people and see what I could learn about the other attendees. What I discovered very quickly was that many of these events did not have my ideal prospects there. In fact, they didn't even have some not-so-ideal prospects. I was not in the right place for my business.

When I got back to my office, I went onto both LinkedIn and MeetUp and found several events where my ideal prospects actually "hung out." Guess what? Talking to people at those events was a lot easier. We all spoke the same language, and I actually enjoyed my time there.

> *Networking without follow-up is a waste of time. Create a system for reaching out to promising contacts to take the conversation further.*

Once I had my perfect pitch down and asked others what they were looking for, the format was fun and so much easier. People were referring me to their peers, and when I asked what other events my prospects attended, I started to attend those, as well. Your circle brings you to more places and people and opportunities.

I also learned that it can be beneficial to hang out with other entrepreneurs. Business owners are a great source of contacts and leads. You will also learn how entrepreneurs think, and their ability to come up with creative solutions as well as their passion for being in business for themselves can rub off on you. Most importantly, you can learn from their successes and failures, especially if they have been working as an entrepreneur longer than you have.

Get Social
Networking does not always have to be face-to-face. You can network online, as well, using social media platforms, like LinkedIn and Google Plus. The key is to approach your online networking efforts in the same way that you do in person, looking for opportunities to bring value to others and help them further their careers, rather than promoting yourself and your abilities.

Choosing the right social networks will depend on

your business and your industry, since not every network is appropriate for every type of venture. Just because you are unfamiliar with how a certain social platform works, however, does not mean you should rule it out. When I first connected with Jason, who is now my online marketing manager, he asked about my presence on social media. I told him about my Facebook page and my LinkedIn account. He asked about Twitter. I told him I was too old to be on Twitter and I didn't care when people were having a cup of coffee. He said to use Twitter as a professional tool and that I needed to have a Twitter account. After a little more goading from his end, I signed up for one.

I made sure to tweet a few times a day, focusing on helpful business tips and words of encouragement. And then, the most unbelievable thing happened. Someone found me on Twitter and asked whether I would speak to their group! When I told Jason, he could have easily said, "I told you so." Instead, he said, "Isn't that awesome?" Wise man.

Embrace the Unfamiliar

My experience with Twitter illustrates an important lesson. Each of us has a preferred way of doing things, whether it's managing our finances, our marketing, or even our supply closet. Maybe those systems work all the time or some of the time, or maybe they used to work but things have changed. Technology has changed. As an entrepreneur, you have to be open to new and wonderful ways of doing things. You have to be open to using different tools and developing new habits to run your business, and even your personal life.

One of those new habits has to do with learning to sing your own praises without reservation. Your mother undoubtedly taught you that bragging is unattractive, and that maxim holds true when the boasting is born of insecurity. As an entrepreneur, however, you have to sell others on your talents and accomplishments. In the next chapter, we'll explore the importance of self-promotion for building your business, and how giving yourself the occasional public pat on the back can make you more attractive to clients.

CHAPTER SIX

TOOT YOUR HORN

Being in business for yourself means you become a one-person marketing machine. Sure, you will have other people and systems to market your products or services. But, when it comes right down to it, if you don't promote yourself, who will?

Thanks to the wonders of the Internet, we literally have the whole world at our fingertips. You can connect with clients and prospects both locally and globally, and sell anything online to anyone, anywhere. If you are really good at marketing yourself, you can attract fans from around the world. When you are first getting your business off the ground, however, odds are most of your sales will happen closer to home. Meeting prospects face-to-face is the most effective way to establish a relationship and ultimately close a sale. Your chances improve if you give them something positive by which to remember you. Here are three strategies that I found fruitful for my own business:

Be the Brand. When people think of you, they should immediately think of your business. You and your product or service should be one and the same in the mind of anyone you have met as an entrepreneur. To accomplish this, consider how you can embody your brand—how you can walk the walk and talk the talk. As an example, my company is Selling in a Skirt. Guess what you will always find me wearing? Yep, a skirt. Spring, summer, fall or winter, regardless of the weather or the occasion, if I am attending a networking event, business conference, or even a private party, I make a point of wearing a skirt to keep my brand consistent. Sometimes, other people show up just to see what I'm wearing! I kept telling everyone my next book would be *Selling in Pajamas,* but at this point, that will have to be book number three.

Create Collateral. When I wrote my first book, I didn't write it with the intention of asking everyone to buy it and make it a best seller. My goal was to pull together the lessons I had learned during 30 years in sales so I could share those insights with others. I sold quite a few, but I also gave them to people that I thought needed to hear my message or needed to meet me. The book became my own version of a business card. Whether you author a book or an eBook, a white paper, or a quick reference guide, creating a tangible resource for prospective clients can position you as a thought-leader and the go-to resource for their needs.

Stay Humble. To promote yourself effectively, you have to be confident. People love to be around confident people, and confidence engenders trust. But, be careful that you don't come across as overly confident or even conceited. Humility is just as attractive as self-assurance, so try to stay a little bit humble. Show gratitude for what you have, never take the people you meet or those that turn into clients for granted, and when your confidence propels you into another level, never forget where you came from.

Letting people know your accomplishments does not have to sound like bragging.

Work the Room

Speaking to Chambers of Commerce and Rotary groups is an excellent strategy to promote your business and connect with well-established professionals in your community. You get a ton of exposure, and you know that these groups are looking for speakers every week or month. When I first started my company, I needed to gain brand awareness. To accomplish this, I would speak anywhere and everywhere I was asked. I was getting my name out and also practicing different talks to see what would become my "signature" talk.

What I ultimately found was that I related quite well to these small groups. As an entrepreneur, I attend meetings frequently and listen to speakers in hopes of learning something that can benefit my business. Sometimes, I will watch to see whether they have a look of disappointment when the attendance is low. Some do and some don't. The smart ones don't because they know, as I do, it's not always the people in the room that can take you elsewhere; it's the people they know.

If you are trying to begin a speaking career, start with the Chamber and Rotary circuit. You get to practice your signature talk and everyone is happy you are there. You will also find that your speaking opportunities start to quickly expand. After only a handful of presentations to Rotary Clubs and Chamber of Commerce meetings, I began getting calls from local and national women's groups, professional associations, male-dominated companies, and even universities asking whether I would come to speak. They wanted to learn about communication. They wanted to bring more women into the fold, and the women wanted to learn how to be taken seriously. I was in a dozen different industries speaking and teaching. I was selling my books and my coaching. Those lunchtime presentations to local groups of 30 to 40 members had blossomed into offers to speak before hundreds at regional and national conferences.

Be Present

Even now that my business is well established, I still speak in front of small groups. Inevitably, someone will ask me why I bother. Isn't it a waste of my time?

The answer is no. Presenting in front of a few dozen people continues to prove beneficial for my business.

Case in point: Several months ago, I agreed to speak to what I knew would be a small group. As the time got closer, I was feeling overwhelmed, because I had so many other things I could have and should have been doing. Giving a brief talk in front of a handful of listeners hardly seemed worth the investment of time. When I arrived at the event, I talked to a few people, had lunch with others, and then got ready to speak.

I only had 30 minutes, but in those 30 minutes I built some amazing relationships. I had listened attentively to the people I met before lunch and shared some of the information I had learned with the audience during my talk. They appreciated the fact that I was able to convey several of their common challenges—they felt that I understood their needs and appreciated the fact that I cared.

Immediately after my presentation, one of the guests approached me to ask whether I could be the keynote speaker at a large convention. I also added two more coaching clients to my business. Many people would have assumed the event had no potential for future business— that it wasn't worth their time. Meanwhile, I scored three new opportunities.

But, wouldn't I rather be talking to an audience of

thousands? I love speaking, period. When I speak to thousands, I connect with a few people at a time, so they feel as if I am talking directly to them. I also feel like I am in a relationship with just them. Whether the room holds five or 5000, to me it's all the same, as long as we are all truly present. So as you look for speaking engagements to build your business, remember:

- You are never wasting your time talking to a small group.

- Remember to do just as much listening as you do talking.

- It's not necessarily the people in the audience that can help you; it's the people they know.

- The people that are supposed to hear your message are the ones that show up.

- You should not despise the day of small beginnings.

Tell the Masses
One of the biggest investments I have made into my business was hiring a PR agency to help with my promotions. My public relations person is Emmy® award-winning reporter Jeff Crilley of RealNews PR. Jeff is all about getting you noticed and helping to market you, your brand and your company. He was instrumental in getting me onto Fox Business News on radio stations throughout the country. Since my first interview, they have called me back on numerous stories and dubbed me their "gender expert." Jeff also wrote a book called *Free Publicity*, which I recommend as an excellent resource

for any entrepreneur just starting out. If you can get news coverage for free, there is no reason *not* to have your name out there! Jeff's book is chock full of information and includes quick tips for free publicity at the end of each chapter. Here are just a few that might get your creative juices flowing:

- Build rapport with reporters. You can never have too many friends in the media.

- Use your expertise for free publicity. Everyone is an expert at something. Search sites like HARO.com (Help a Reporter Out) for opportunities to be interviewed as a subject matter expert.

- Be available. Reporters will go back to the same sources over and over as long as they deliver.

- Write a press release. Craft a headline that you can imagine reading in the paper, and write the copy as if it were going to be read on air.

Market Smarter

If PR is not your thing, you can use plenty of other grassroots marketing strategies to promote your business and your brand. Here are four quick tips to help generate movement in your business:

1. **Sponsor an event at your office.** Invite potential clients and strategic partners to see what you are all about.

2. **Create electronic versions of your brochures.** Prospects will be able to download the materials instantly from your website.

3. **Identify walking ambassadors.** Find a group of friends and colleagues who are willing to evangelize for your business. They will tell everyone they meet about you, so you can harness the power of referrals.

4. **Give away information.** Create an opt-in section on your website and offer a free report rather than a newsletter. This will help build your list and get your name out as a valuable resource for timely information.

Depending on which strategies you are using for self-promotion, you might even consider plotting everything out on a marketing calendar. Maybe you are releasing a new product and plan to announce it using a press release prior to the launch. Maybe your book will be ready before an event and you can use social media to generate early buzz with event participants. And maybe you just want to shine a little light on your business by writing a blog post. Using a calendar to decide what kind of marketing you will do and when provides a great visual tool to help you stay organized.

Use speaking engagements, press releases, articles and social media posts to promote your business.

At this point, you know the value of getting your

name out, meeting people, and creating "buzz." Now, you are ready to tackle one of the biggest challenges an entrepreneur will face—one that will make or break your business.

When you work for an employer, you keep regular hours and have a set routine. You get up in the morning, go to the office, spend your day doing your job, drive home, and go to sleep. Lather, rinse and repeat. But what happens when nobody else is calling the shots or making you punch the clock? How do you create structure out of chaos?

CHAPTER SEVEN

RULE THE DAY

What is the first thing nearly everyone says when you tell them you are working from home? "Wow! You're so lucky!"

They assume that you can finish all of the projects on your chore list because you work where you live. Your meals are all cooked and your laundry is done and you have tackled the myriad of minor home repairs that need fixing, right? Well, if that is the way you are planning on working from home, then I will be the first one to tell you, "Go get a real job." You can't succeed long-term if you mix your personal life with your professional life.

Time management is one of the hardest concepts entrepreneurs have to grasp, especially when it means working from home. Many people find the transition from an office routine to the self-employed lifestyle confusing, because there are no rules. The only person holding you accountable to putting in a full day's work is you, and the desire to procrastinate is ever-present.

I have been working from home for almost 30 years, so it is second nature to me. The key is to establish structure in both your day and your environment, so you can focus on work without distraction. By developing a few new habits, you will quickly get into a groove to run your business successfully, whether from the spare bedroom down the hall or the coffee shop down the street.

Act As If

First things first: You should get up every morning as if you had an office to go to outside your home. The key phrase here is *as if*. Live your life as if, and soon it will be. Be prepared and be professional. Now, I'm not saying you need to wear a suit or put on heels and stylish accessories before taking on the day's projects. I'm saying you have to be ready to get in a professional mode.

Even though you may not physically see your clients and prospects, they can tell when you are play working. (What is play working? It's when you pretend you are working—you play like you have a job—but you're just doing busy work and nothing productive is happening.) With the introduction of Skype, Zoom and Google Plus, you never know when a client will ask you to get on a video call. Wouldn't that be great if you look like you rolled out of bed?

I will be the first to admit that I love my "sweats" days. Although my brand is Selling in a Skirt, when I have a big work project I need to get done, I stay in my sweats all day, throw on a baseball cap, and hunker down in my home office for hours at a time. Those are the most productive days for me. Writing my books took place on many of those days. But, there is a difference between "sweats" days during the week and those on the weekend. During the week, I still don't have to leave the house, but at least I've put on some light makeup and run a brush through my hair. I may have no intention of being seen in public, but that doesn't mean a client or prospect won't decide to ring me up for a Google Hangout. Always be prepared to put your best face forward, even on the fly.

> *Effective time management is critical to your success as an entrepreneur. Act as if you have a boss to avoid distractions and stay focused on your work.*

Set Boundaries

Throughout my business career, I've told anyone that I have trained that they need to set boundaries and expectations for their family, as well as for themselves. More men have failed in their own businesses not because they lack the talent or skill, but because they have a "honey do" list constantly thrown in their face. Women often fail because their husbands will complain about dinner not being ready at a normal hour, even though, "You were home all day."

Let your family know when you are working and when you can take a break. When I worked in insurance, one of my male producers would wear a hat to signify his current work status. When that hat was on, his children knew he was working and did not bother him. Hat off, and daddy is home. I also knew a woman who had a glass door on her home office and a sign with a clock letting her children know when she would be available to them. Setting boundaries may be uncomfortable at first, but once everyone gets used to the new routine, your productivity will increase substantially.

Be Accountable

Of course, emergencies and exceptions always come up, and not everyone follows the rules. But, like in any other process, failure to set expectations is an invitation to chaos. Not only do you have to state your expectations, you have to have them, as well. As the great philosopher and theologian Albert Schweitzer once said, "You must not expect anything from others. It's you, of yourself, of whom you must ask a lot. Only from oneself has one the right to ask everything and anything. This way it's up to you...your own choices...what you get from others remains a present, a gift."

Pace Yourself

With all of that said, be careful not to swing the pendulum the other way and work without an end in sight. Working from home makes it very easy to sit down at the computer in the evening to start a project or an article or a book or whatever and just work into the wee hours of the morning. I succumbed to this cycle more times than I care to admit, each time rationalizing it by thinking that no one would miss me since I was actually home, or telling myself that everyone was asleep, so it didn't matter if I worked in the middle of the night. It does matter, and before you know it, you are working 90 hours a week without a lot to show for it.

Focus on work, but remember to play.

Put it on Paper

When I first started working from home 30 years ago, I developed a highly effective system to schedule work, family and everything in between. I still use the system today. If you are a high-tech kind of person, please ask that part of your brain to take a brief nap—it is not needed for this system.

First, purchase a blotter-sized calendar. You need a calendar that you can see without having to turn on a computer or phone. One that is made of paper. Big paper.

Next, grab several markers in different colors. If you are a parent, write down on the calendar every activity that your children are involved in before or after school, including start and stop times. (Using different colors for each child will make it easy to distinguish who is going where when.) If you don't have children, skip this step.

Take another marker and do the same exercise for your spouse or partner, and then finally for yourself. Every personal activity goes on the calendar, including gym time, pedicures, dentist appointments, piano lessons, book club, etc.

Grab another marker and put down those appointments that are set for your work. Will you be attending a training seminar or conference? Do you have to meet with your lawyer or accountant? Do you have a set day to check in with your virtual assistant? When is your weekly mastermind group call? Anything work-related that needs your attention goes on the schedule.

At this point, you can see clearly which time slots are completely gone and which are available. But, you're not done yet. One of the biggest mistakes entrepreneurs make is not considering marketing as an activity or appointment. Marketing is imperative for entrepreneurs. When you worked in a corporate environment, you picked up your phone and your Marketing Department handled it. Now, you are the Marketing Department...and the Sales, Accounting, Maintenance, IT, and Operations Departments, too. Schedule time to do marketing as if it were a business meeting. You wouldn't miss a meeting with a client, so why would you miss the one activity that will bring in revenue? Get it on the calendar!

Finally, make a commitment to follow your calendar and be flexible only when necessary. And make sure you look at your calendar every morning. *Yes, every morning!*

I've been using the calendar method for three decades, and I promise you, it will help you stay focused and give you better control of your time management. As an added bonus, your family will know when you are working and when you aren't. They can see when you are in a meeting and when you are attending their soccer game—and your children will know they are important enough to make it onto your calendar. It's a win-win situation for everyone.

Remember, if you want other people to value your time, you must value it first. Set boundaries, schedule important events, and establish a routine. Get the most from every minute of the day.

Keep Your Promises

Part of managing your schedule also involves fulfilling your commitments. Without a boss looking over your shoulder, you may be inclined to let things slide in some areas (especially if you're really, really busy). Trust me when I say that a lackadaisical attitude about deadlines and commitments quickly will bite you on the backside.

When you are in business for yourself, you must be mindful of the fact that people trust what you tell them. If you say you are going to call someone on Tuesday, you need to call them on Tuesday. If you say that you are going to send them information that night, then before your head hits the pillow, make sure you send that information out to them. Not everyone in business is that forthcoming and backs up their word. If you lack integrity in this area, however, you will soon find yourself lacking new clients.

Case in point: Some time ago, I received an email from a speaker and coach inviting me to a webinar that week. As a speaker and a trainer, I am always on the quest to learn from people in the same line of work, to help me grow my business. I absolutely knew that the information that was the focus of the webinar would be tremendously helpful, and I promptly registered. At the end of the webinar, the coordinator extended an invitation for a 1:1 session with the speaker. Participants needed to fill out an online request form with their contact details, and we were notified that we had a good possibility of being chosen *if* we were at the right level in our business.

I was very excited to learn later that I had been selected. A phone appointment was set for the following week, and I couldn't wait. Two days before the appointment, I received an email from the speaker's office. Her assistant wanted to make sure I had the correct time and call in number, and that we both were prepared for the call's agenda. Two final questions were listed with the disclaimer that the responses to these final questions would have no impact on the call and I was not required to purchase anything at all. The only request in the notification was that I respond as quickly as possible, which I did.

After originally having been told that I qualified for the 1:1 consultation, I promptly received another email that said they had determined I was not a viable candidate to take up the speaker's time. She was way too busy, the email explained. So my appointment was cancelled. Little did they know, so was I.

I was beyond annoyed and decided to send an email directly to the speaker. I explained the entire situation from my perspective and closed with, "I wish you continued success and so sorry you don't feel beginning a relationship with me or my company is worth your while." Within minutes of hitting Send, I received a reply from her office letting me know that they didn't really mean to cancel—they meant to reschedule.

Guess who didn't respond? I can learn from plenty of other speakers and trainers and have no desire to work with someone who is so flippant about building relationships, or so careless with my calendar. Remember, *everyone* is strapped for time. Be careful what you promise. It's always better to under-promise and over-deliver rather than the other way around. Women are known to refer people, businesses and information 92 percent of the time. Bet you can guess who isn't getting any referrals from this woman.

Time is precious, both yours and that of your clients and prospects. Managing your time wisely and setting appropriate priorities is fundamental to your business success. In the next chapter, we will take the idea of valuing your time a step further by ascribing a dollar amount to the unique expertise you have to offer.

Define Success

Entrepreneurs are passionate people, and your level of passion and drive can be a good predictor of your future success. Ultimately, it comes down to whether you can earn a living, of course. But the gratification you experience in running your own business also points to just how successful you are and what lies ahead. After all, you're far less likely to realize a financial gain if you are not wholeheartedly committed to your business.

I've always said that when you do something, you should dedicate yourself to it 100 percent. Whether you are a veteran or a newbie, you have to play full out. Money is a strong motivator, of course, but I have found that setting my own standard of success has helped propel me forward throughout my career. I have given my all in every endeavor, because I determined what constituted a personal "win."

When I was selling, others viewed the money I earned as the measure of my success. I was more interested in the recognition. Either way, I was successful. When I was an Agency Manager, my report card was based on the number of recruits I brought in. I measured my success by the recruits that came in, stayed and became producers. Either way, I was successful. When I delivered training, the surveys came back with all high scores, based to some extent on the fact that the attendees liked me. I would look at the future increase in their bottom lines. Either way, I was successful.

As you embark on your new enterprise, think about what kind of accomplishments or feedback would define your success on a personal level. Then, keep your eye on the prize, and commit your very best effort to achieving that goal.

Remember to Live

When I left my corporate gig in the insurance industry, I had a pretty good life. Let me rephrase that. Professionally, I had a pretty good life. I was protecting clients with policies, I was guiding employees to new opportunities in their career, and I was being recognized as a valued leader. On top of that, I was making a lot of money. The downside was that I was working around the clock. The rewards were obvious, but my personal life was non-existent.

When I decided to start my own business, I wanted to

achieve more balance between my work and my life. The stress of my hectic schedule combined with the lack of a social life had compelled me to leave Corporate America, and I did not want to repeat those habits when I started working for myself. At the same time, I knew that the start-up phase of any business is the toughest part. I was prepared to do whatever it took to launch my new career, so I rolled up my sleeves and dug right in.

My first two years as a speaker, author and trainer were a whirlwind of excitement. I made incredible contacts, and my business got off to a very good start. But when the dust started to settle, I knew I was missing something. I was repeating the patterns that I had in the corporate job that I quit to start my own business in the first place, working 20-hour days and isolating myself from friends and associates because I was consumed with the business. Even though I was networking, I spent most of my time alone, putting together training programs and presentations and marketing materials, often working late into the night.

In short, I was so busy being an entrepreneur, I had forgotten to have a personal life.

My priorities were no better than they were when I was selling insurance. In fact, they were worse. I decided to have a heart-to-heart with myself, turned off the computer, and sat quietly as I pondered my situation. Was I still doing what I believe I was called to do? Did I still love it? Was I missing anything? Was I consumed with worry about my shrinking bank account?

Here's what I discovered:

- I still loved what I was doing and, if I could do it for free, I would be happy.

- I did feel I was making a difference, which is vital.

- I was missing a personal life, and if I continued the way I was doing it, I would never find one.

- And yes, I was concerned about my dwindling funds, but working more wasn't going to change that.

I realized that I needed to make some changes and to have more balance between work and play. You should, too. Life is way too short. No one lies on their deathbed wishing that they had worked harder. You want to make a difference, yes, but that doesn't mean you have to sacrifice yourself on the altar of entrepreneurship. I know I make a difference in people's lives every day, especially in the lives of my sweet mentees. (We'll discuss the merits of becoming a mentor later in the book.) Ultimately, being successful as an entrepreneur is more than just earning a good income, it's about being happy.

Enjoy the Ride
Lest you think that setting aside some time for your social life will be a hindrance to your business success, let me tell you a story that may offer some encouragement. Once I committed to making my personal life a priority again, remarkable new doors of opportunity began to open for me. The most notable one occurred right after I gave the keynote speech to a group of young women

about to graduate from college. In the audience was a woman on the event committee, with whom I quickly became friends. We met for lunch or coffee on a regular basis. One day she asked whether I would be interested in helping out with sales training for a company that her brother-in-law ran. As we know in sales, referrals are the most expensive "free" lead, and you need to covet them. I said, "Of course." She then told me the training was for engineers. Seriously? Engineers take to sales like a fish to a bicycle, but again, I said of course. "One more thing," she added...they were mostly retired military.

I envisioned delivering the sales training to a group of humorless, regimented, uptight men who had little interest in the subject matter to begin with. But, a referral is precious, and I trusted my friend would not steer me wrong.

I steeled my resolve, reiterated my desire to move forward and promptly began putting together mental notes for my meeting with the company president, a retired Air Force Colonel.

Be flexible. Opportunities aren't always gift-wrapped.

(Before I continue this story, I want to quickly point out that even though you have a picture of your ideal client and you are laser-beam focused on your niche, sometimes a new and different client is presented to you. Engineers were not in my niche category; however, the training that they needed and the communication styles they needed to understand were, so I embraced the opportunity.)

I could share all the details of what happened at our first meeting, the training I did for the group of sales-minded engineers, and the positive feedback I received on the materials that I had put together for the company. But, let me cut to the chase. I was fired.

You see, during the term of my contract, the Colonel and I became friends. Great friends. And, as it happens, he had something more in mind. He explained that he was firing me because he wanted to date me. I told him two things: First, I've never been fired before, and second, he had better make it worth my while. He did, we dated, and within a year's time, we got married. To top it all off, his team still uses my ideas and the women in his company still contact me for coaching and mentoring. See how making room for your personal life can actually benefit your business?

Remember, as an entrepreneur, you have to be flexible. Yes, you need to have a very clear concept of your target audience and structure in your daily routine—but you also need to have fun, and embrace the unique opportunities that present themselves as you get your business off the ground. In the next chapter, we'll explore a few other strategies to grow revenues and establish meaningful relationships with clients and strategic partners.

FAMOUS ISN'T ENOUGH: EARNING YOUR FORTUNE AS AN ENTREPRENEUR

CHAPTER EIGHT

SELL THE COW

Female readers may remember a lesson their mother or sister taught them as they were entering womanhood. "Why would a man buy the cow when he can get the milk for free?" This maxim holds true for entrepreneurs, as well.

When you are just starting out, you want people to discover you and like you. You are willing to offer your services for a pittance, or ask for nothing at all, because you are grateful for the opportunity to showcase your talents. But, eventually, you have to put food in the fridge.

The first couple of years that I was promoting myself as a sales trainer specializing in gender communications, I got plenty of buzz. Everywhere I was scheduled to speak, people were so excited to hear me. They had heard from others how amazing I was and how accessible I was and on and on. The information I was giving was relevant to them, and I was excited how my new career was progressing. Even people who had heard me before said they learned something new when I came back to speak to their group. I was relatable, and I was funny.

Yet, I wasn't monetizing my talks. I would talk about my book and have copies with me and even sold a few here and there, but it wasn't generating revenue. I was giving a lot of bang for not very much buck.

A friend who is a business consultant asks each of his clients, "What keeps you up at night?" He follows it with, "Who helps you with that?" When I first launched my consulting venture, my concerns were very clear: I needed income. I kept thinking, if I'm as awesome as everyone says I am, why am I not booked solid with training, coaching and speaking? I give some pretty impressive information and break it down so that people can start implementing it right away and I'm available to help solve their challenges.

Rein It In

Eventually, I realized that I was too accessible. Of course, initially I thought that being readily available was a great thing. Why wouldn't I want to respond to emails from potential clients or talk on the phone or have a brainstorming session together? I was everywhere and people liked to be around me. The problem was, they could hear me share valuable insights and strategies without paying for it. I had to ask myself, "How do I change my behavior to be more of a businesswoman and less of a friend?"

People also didn't really understand how I made money. They thought I must be earning big fees from my public speaking or making huge royalties from my book or that I was independently wealthy. Whatever they thought, they assumed that I was ultra-successful. Meanwhile, I was still struggling to get my new business off the ground, even after the first two years. Maybe it was the way I carried myself or the way I dressed, but the fact that I looked like a million bucks actually seemed to be keeping the money at bay. Again, I had to ask myself how to change my behavior—I needed to be more forthcoming about finances without telling anyone my bank account was dwindling.

> *Be willing to speak for free when you are first starting out, but remember that you are a for-profit business.*

I started planting seeds in my talks about my work and my worth. For instance, I would tell a story about a client who had me on retainer, or I would talk about the fact that I was working with someone as their business coach. This way, people would hear and understand that I am compensated by being hired for coaching or training or speaking. This new approach started working immediately, and I knew I was on to something. I had to stop giving away the milk and communicate the value of the cow.

Determine Your Worth

If you are just starting your business, you need to set your rates. If you own a retail venture, that means not only pricing your products, but also pricing your time, so that you can earn a living wage from the profits. If you are a consultant or other service-provider, you need to establish your fees and decide whether and how you will accommodate special requests from clients, such as a retainer agreement or long-term contract.

Your competition will have an impact on the value of your product or service, but several other factors also come into play. The economic means of your target audience, your professional background and industry experience, and even your geographical location will influence your pricing. With these factors in mind, how do you begin to formulate your rates?

One way to determine your pricing is by setting an income goal and estimated work schedule, and then working backward to calculate your fee. For example, let's say that in the first year, you hope to earn $75,000 in income, or $6,250/month. To get your business off the ground, you expect to work 60 hours a week. First, calculate how many hours a month you will be working:

$$(60 \text{ hours/week x } 52 \text{ weeks}) / 12 \text{ months} = 260 \text{ hours/month}$$

Now, divide your target monthly income by the number of hours you will be working to get your hourly rate:

$$\$6{,}250 / 260 = \$24.04/\text{hour}$$

Of course, you will not be paid for every hour that you work. For example, if you are a personal trainer, you will only be paid for the time that you actually spend training clients. However, you will still need to invest many more hours of your time to market your business, meet with prospects and referrals, research exercise and nutrition studies, etc. How do you get paid for the rest of the time you are working? In this case, you need to set a target for how many hours you can feasibly meet with clients, and adjust your rates accordingly.

Let's say that you believe you can train five clients a day on Monday – Saturday for a one-hour training session. That means you will be training for 30 hours/week. With that in mind, run your calculation again, replacing the 60-hour workweek with a 30-hour week. (You will still be working 60 hours, but you will only be earning income for the 30 hours you are training clients.)

$$(30 \text{ hours/week} \times 52 \text{ weeks}) / 12 \text{ months} =$$
$$130 \text{ hours/month}$$

$$\$6{,}250 / 130 = \$48.08/\text{hour}$$

After running these calculations, you may determine that \$50/hour is a better rate to achieve your income goals. If you research the competition, you will also find that your rate falls within the average range for personal trainers in your area.

If you don't know what to charge for your services, check out the competition.

Accommodate Exceptions

What if you're in a different line of work—say, a graphic designer—and a client wants to put you on retainer? Your standard rate is $75/hour. For a 40-hour workweek, that comes out to $3,000/week, which is more than your client wants to spend. How much should you adjust your fee?

To calculate the answer, go back to your original equation. When you set your rate at $75/hour, you may have assumed that you would only be actively working on client projects for 30 hours/week. The rest of the time, you would be doing social media marketing, reading industry blogs for the latest trends, and attending networking meetings. So, if your rate of $75/hour was based on a 30-hour week, your target was $2,250/week. If you are on retainer for a 40-hour week, your hourly rate would drop to $56.25/hour ($2,250 / 40 = $56.25). You can offer a lower fee to your client, while still meeting your own income goal.

As an entrepreneur, sometimes you do have to be flexible, but don't let a client strong-arm you into slashing your rates (even if they try to sway you with flattery). When I established my fees, I gave myself my bottom line—I wouldn't do this for less than that. I wouldn't leave my house for less than a certain amount. I wouldn't travel and train for less than X. Know what your "X" is, and you can have conversations about your fees with confidence.

Negotiate Like a Pro

Once I set my standard rates and my minimums, I felt

like I had reached a milestone as an entrepreneur. I was working on my terms and not anyone else's. When someone said they did not have a large budget, my next question would be, "What did you pay your last speaker or trainer?" If they said they did not have the funds available for training or speaking, I would ask them to purchase my book for all the attendees and we would work on a smaller fee. Sometimes, if the group is one that I know I should be in front of and the prospect has no budget at all, I will agree to waive my fee if they will introduce me to 3-5 clients that need my services.

No matter how you determine your rates, *write them down*—both before and after you negotiate with a client. Don't try to memorize your fees or remember what you quoted someone or the deal you struck in the back of the room. Put everything on paper. Otherwise, an amicable conversation can turn into a "he said, she said" scenario, and even if you're hired, no one will feel good about where you landed.

A friend of mine who is a speaker also told me, you have to be able to say what your rates are without totally cracking up. For instance, she says, "My fee is $25,000 and here is what is included..." She admits it took her a number of times before she could state her fee without either choking on the number or laughing until the tears were rolling, but she can now tell her clients what she is worth and stands behind that number.

Drive New Business
With your pricing in place and boundaries set, your job now is to get in front of enough people, share your

message, strengthen your brand, and become the person that customers want to buy from and companies are looking to hire. Remember, everyone started the same way: unknown. At this stage, though, you can no longer sell yourself short. You just have to sell yourself! Success may not happen overnight, but with consistency and tenacity, it will. (Haven't you ever heard of someone being labeled an overnight sensation only to find out they had been toiling in obscurity for 10 years prior?)

At this point in your launch, you have defined your target audience, established a clear brand message, surrounded yourself with a strong support team, created a savvy marketing plan, and implemented a well-structured work routine. You are on your way! The key, now, is to stay motivated, focused and committed to meeting your goals. Owning your own business can be a rollercoaster ride, and in the same way that you experience exhilarating highs, you can encounter unexpected setbacks that will set your heart racing. In the next chapter, we'll take a look at how to overcome adversity and get back on track to achieve your dreams as an entrepreneur.

CHAPTER NINE

PLAN OR PERISH

The ups and downs of being an entrepreneur can take its toll on you. You spend hundreds of hours trying to get noticed, and when you finally start to gain traction in your business, life turns into an episode of *Project Runway*. One day you're in and the next day you're out. Throughout all the ups and downs, you have to keep your eye on the prize. Go back and review your initial goals and objectives. Have they changed? Have you added to them? Is the business still your passion? No matter what, things change. As pastor and author Charles Swindoll so eloquently said, "Life is 10 percent what happens to you and 90 percent how you react to it."

I always find it interesting to learn how and why people throw in the towel. When I was selling insurance, most of us wanted to quit every other day. Some did. In my mind, there was no room for failure. If you wanted to get something done and you couldn't do it yourself, find someone that could help. Bring in the big guns, but don't quit. As an entrepreneur, to be successful, you have to be excited and passionate about what you do...every day.

Otherwise, you will have a new title—business owner—
and at that point, maybe being in Corporate America was
the better choice.

Be prepared for the highs and lows in your business.

I'm not saying you have to be happy and peppy
every day, but you need to have a positive outlook more
days than not. With that said, sometimes, no matter how
hard you try, how many years of expertise you may have
and how much time you gave it, there comes a time when
you have to call it a day. While starting a business is hard,
closing one is harder. Your ego and pride start to protest.
What will people think and say? You might think your
latest undertaking was just another failure to add to your
list, but that isn't the case. The fact is, not all ventures are
successful. That doesn't mean your efforts were in vain.
The trick is to time the closure well so that you can cut
your losses, take what you learned, and move forward.

Prepare for Adversity

Of course, my goal with this book is to help you avoid
that scenario. And the two best ways to ensure that you
never have to face the pain of involuntarily shuttering
your business are by planning ahead and pushing through.

We have talked a lot about planning already, including
the need to plan your budget, your promotional strategy,

and your schedule. The more upfront planning you do, the more likely you are to achieve your short- and long-term goals, and the less likely you are to be thrown off course as you build your business. But planning is more than just logistical considerations; it includes changing your mindset and putting checks and balances in place to get you back on track when challenges arise.

Believe in Yourself

No matter how much planning you do, hard times will come. That is not only the nature of business, but the nature of the world at large. Economies go up and down. Technology changes the playing field. New competitors come along, who are faster or less expensive. In the big picture, none of those scenarios needs to lead to shutting down your business; instead, you must find ways to adapt and find the strength to keep on keepin' on.

A book that is a must read for every entrepreneur is *Three Feet From Gold* by Sharon Lechter and Greg Reid. The title comes from the concept of someone who has been digging in a mineshaft for years and then throws in the towel, when it turns out they were only three feet away from the vein of gold that would have made them a millionaire.

The book conveys an important lesson, based on the life of Napoleon Hill: "The most common cause of failure is quitting. Success always follows a similar pattern...First comes a dream, followed by struggle, and then there is victory. The problem is, most people give up in the struggle section and never get to sense what victory feels like."

I have started over and recreated myself on many occasions. I've been very successful and have the accolades to prove that. But, I have never been as passionate about anything as I am with my company. Rather than digging in a mineshaft, I am working every day to promote my business and build relationships, adjusting goals when needed but staying in the game. That gold truly is just three feet away. Believing in yourself is the only answer. I have always said and will continue to believe that failure is not an option. When something isn't working, you may need to give in a bit, but don't give up. To help you regain perspective, you should periodically evaluate:

- What do you know that you know?

- What do you know that you don't know?

- What do you think you know?

- What do others know that you don't know?

These simple questions may reveal some pertinent answers to foster your success.

Avoid Shiny Objects
Some setbacks happen because of external circumstances—a dip in the economy, a new marketing campaign from a competitor, a flu that takes you out of commission for two weeks. Other setbacks can be of your own creation, which was the case with me during the second year of my new venture. The story is a long one, which only illustrates just how far off course you can go when you start to pursue an opportunity that is not part of

your core business strategy.

The seed was planted during a phone call with a friend. We were talking about ways to expand our respective businesses, and he mentioned that membership sites were the "it" thing. The concept sounded intriguing, and I started visualizing what I could offer as a subscription-based program. I had just finished a series of workbooks that brought sales professionals through the entire sales process. If we added some audio and video files and downloadable PDFs, I thought, we could create an online curriculum.

I knew that I could call on my Dream Team to do what I either did not want to do or didn't know how to do. My expertise is in sales, not IT, so I would need their help. But, PJ and Jason let me know that the project was not in their field of expertise either. Undaunted, I looked for other options. The vision was so clear in my head, I couldn't just abandon it without even trying.

I asked several people for referrals and a very successful friend told me about an unbelievable designer who builds membership sites. He made the introduction and we scheduled a Skype call. That's when I found out he lived in Europe. The designer assured me that technology would make communications easy. He said he found my idea intriguing but noted that he really didn't want to take on any new clients and needed to sleep on it.

Turns out in the IT world, "sleeping on it" means taking a week to decide. Fortunately, his decision was that he wanted to work with me. Better yet, during his week-long hibernation, he had come up with several ideas. His vision and mine were beginning to gel. We talked about costs and time and he told me what he thought I could expect financially and all was amazing—until he backed out three weeks later when we were just about to sign the contract. He had changed his mind about taking on another client. Since he was successful in his field, he could pick and choose his projects, and ultimately mine was not a priority. I felt like the air was taken out of the room. In those three weeks I had come up with financial projections based on his ideas—projections that I feared would not become reality.

The following week, I spoke at a networking event. In the audience was a designer who worked for a company that did online membership sites. Was this fate? Should I try again? What's the worst that could happen? I decided to take the plunge and we set up a 1:1 meeting. After hearing the idea, the situation I had just been through, and the price tag I was quoted, he told me he would get back to me with a proposal within 24 hours. Surprisingly, he did.

The bigger surprise was the cost—double what Contestant Number One had quoted. When I told him how shocked I was, he explained how professional his company was and all of the things they could do for the membership site (none of which were included in the bid). I told him thanks but no thanks. And that's when he pulled the rug out from under me: He cut the price in half.

Red flags shot up all over the place. I asked how

he could reduce the rate so dramatically. He said that he really wanted my business. So, if I had agreed 10 minutes earlier he would have taken the money? I thanked him and bid him farewell. Now, I was even more frustrated and upset.

Although my faith in humanity was crushed, I was given another referral and decided to meet with yet another program designer. He seemed knowledgeable and kind and told me everything I wanted to hear—this project would be his priority, he could see the vision, we were on the same page, we would create an online resource for sales people. I was hooked.

I won't go into all the gory details, but let's just say that I dedicated an obscene amount of money and time to the project, and 11 months later—nine months longer than it should have taken—I pulled the plug and put it into a medically induced coma. I don't know whether it will ever be awakened, but I am absolutely sure that shutting it down was the right move, physically, emotionally and professionally. (Financially is another story.)

Contrary to what you might think, the problem was not the fact that I had partnered with a program designer who couldn't get the job done. The problem was that my core business took a major hit, because I was focusing all my time and energy trying to launch another venture, before my first one was even concrete. Remember the Strategic Triangle? Although the membership site was related to my work as a sales trainer, writing an online curriculum was not within my three areas of focus. If it feels like you are spinning your wheels in your business, refer back to your Strategic Triangle or original business plan to make sure your efforts still are focused on your original goals.

Follow the Recipe

Another common cause of stagnation in a new business is when the owner starts fiddling with the recipe. I believe that, no matter what industry they are in, every entrepreneur is in sales. And in my experience, salespeople often want to continually "tweak" things to get a better outcome. The irony is that when something already works, they change it. Here's a story that happened many years ago, which can serve as a good example of what unnecessary changes can do to your business.

I had brought a new producer to the team. He was a really nice man, married with children, and had the best hair on the planet. I know that sounds funny, but it was the kind of hair that made both men and women jealous. His hair was the greatest ice-breaker because everyone commented on it. He had some difficulty passing the exam for his insurance license, but he was persistent and finally earned his credentials. He came out of the gate like a rocket. He was selling and educating and building relationships and reaching his milestones, and we were all really proud of him.

Then one week, he turned in no business. He said that nothing went right that week, but he would have a good week the following week. The next week, he turned in another zero. When I asked what happened on his appointments, he said nothing went right that week, but he would have a good week the following week. So now we are in week three and—yep, you guessed it—another big fat zero. Something was going on. I asked him what he had changed, and he said nothing. I knew that was not accurate. If nothing had changed, what happened to his results?

Finally, after more questioning, we were able to peel back the onion. He said he was tired of doing business the way he was doing it. He wanted to be just like my number one producer and thought by mimicking him, he would reap the rewards. Problem was, the two men were nothing alike—not only in looks (picture DeVito and Schwarzenegger in the movie *Twins*), but in personalities. I mean, *nothing* alike. I tried to explain to him that people bought from him because they trusted him and that I would bet that if he went back to being him, all would be good. He did, and it was.

The lesson here? When something is working, don't change it.

Get Refocused

Whether the setback in your business was due to external forces or a bad judgment call, you can't let it stop your forward momentum. Your first priority is to get back on track quickly. And, the best way to accomplish this is with the help of a strategist.

Your strategist may be your business coach, a fellow entrepreneur, or a friend who is good at big-picture planning. Mine was Chris Feola. He walked me through a powerful strategy session that helped me refocus my mind back onto my core business. Here's how it worked:

Stick four poster-size Post It® Notes on the wall.

Write a different heading on each one: **Money, Marketing, Admin** and **Other**.

- Money is anything that can and will make you money, such as working on a client project.

- Marketing is anything that you do to build your business, like posting on social media or speaking at a Chamber of Commerce event.

- Admin is anything you have to do to keep your business running, like paying bills and filing taxes.

- Other is anything that doesn't fit in the other three categories.

Consider every piece of your business and list it under one or more of these headings. Everything had to be on one of the lists.

Walking through this exercise with Chris took a couple of hours, because I wanted to make sure I didn't leave anything out. Finally, I ended up with six items on my Money list, 12 in Marketing, five under Admin, and nothing in the Other column. Chris gently prodded me to add a few things to the Other list, because these are the items would be moving around to get me "focused."

After a few hours, we came up with my final list. I now had three things under Money list, four in Marketing, five in Admin and five under Other. Some of the items I had listed previously were now gone completely.

> *Strategizing with a coach or another entrepreneur can help you get back to your original vision.*

What's the purpose of this exercise? To keep you from getting distracted and help you stay focused on the core activities that will benefit your business. You need to be strict, and it's best to find someone who can hold you accountable. I recommend doing the exercise with a business coach or experienced entrepreneur to help guide your thinking, but you can use the worksheet below to gain some preliminary perspective on your own business activities. If you want to take something off the "Other" list, you have to also eliminate something off another list. Likewise, focus on building your network horizontally before adding any more products or services vertically. You may be inclined to keep building vertically to enhance your product offering, rather than building your network horizontally so that when you do launch a product, you have more than your 12 closest friends buying it.

BUSINESS ACTIVITIES EXERCISE

MONEY	MARKETING	ADMIN	OTHER

Find an Ally

Even though the strategy session took place almost a year ago, it is never far from my mind and vision. What was left on my Money list ultimately became my Strategic Triangle for speaking, training and coaching. I have a picture of my Strategic Triangle in my office, on my phone, on my desk and near my "paper" calendar. Why? As I just shared, I am a shiny object person. If something looks interesting, I will be tempted to add it to my list. Why have a Strategic Triangle when you can have a six-sided strategic hexagon? This is where having an accountability partner comes in.

Your accountability partner is someone who will call you out in an instant and not feel guilty about it, because they truly want you to succeed. They are someone who understands the structure of your business, knows your goals, and is able to speak from experience to offer wise council. As an entrepreneur, you *must* have one or two of these people in your world. And, you have to check your ego at the door. Hearing constructive criticism (and sometimes tough love) is never easy, but ask yourself this question, "If I go astray, what am I giving up?" We all need someone who can help us to see the forest for the trees.

Remember, athletes have coaches, and even coaches have coaches. Isn't that just another word for an accountability partner? In the next chapter, we'll look at how you can be that ally and coach to other budding entrepreneurs. Success is even sweeter when it's shared!

CHAPTER TEN

PAY IT FORWARD

I was very successful in my previous career; yet, as I think back over my 30 years in sales, I recognized that a key element was missing. I wondered whether others felt the same about their own professional journey and conducted an informal poll of professionals in my circle of influence. When asked what would have been a game-changer for their career, the answer was unanimous: a mentor.

I was fortunate to have numerous male mentors who were among the best in the business. Even with those role models, a girl can only be a girl. I tried my best to "man" up, but as a woman, you simply cannot learn everything, "copy" everything, or become like your male mentor. I was either teased because I would ask so many questions or I was ridiculed for taking so long to make friends with clients, or hit on because they thought I was cute. None of these scenarios were flattering or easy to take. But, trudge along I did.

What I was missing was a female mentor. Although I learned a lot from male colleagues who helped guide my career path, ultimately, men and women speak a different language. I was always on the lookout for a female mentor, and they were in woefully short supply.

When I ventured out as an entrepreneur, I knew that I wanted to help other young women just starting out. The idea struck me, like a neon light flashing in my mind: MENTOR. The question was, how do you accomplish this outside of a corporate environment? Where do find someone who will appreciate your experience and need your guidance? In some cases, you just show up and let fate run its course. In other instances, you may need to take a more structured approach.

Embrace Happenstance

My first mentee came to me by way of kismet. A few years ago, while at a networking event geared toward independent business owners, I met a young woman named Fanny who was being mentored by a male friend of mine. My friend asked whether I had any interest in being the "unofficial" mentor to this young woman to give her the female perspective on entrepreneurship. I was so excited and when I first met with Fanny one-on-one, it was instant love. She was going to be graduating college within a few months and had lots of questions. She was bright and personable, and she soaked up information like a little sponge. Over the course of several months, we talked and shared and became friends. When she graduated, I felt like a proud momma. She quickly found an internship with an accounting firm in San Francisco, and her career is off to a strong start. Although it has been a few years since that first meeting, Fanny knows that if she needs anything or just wants to talk, I'm there for her.

I met two more young protégés in a similar fashion at other networking events. At one, a young woman stole the spotlight. She wasn't the type to demand attention, but she lit up the room with her confidence and intelligence. Earlina was in charge of the sales team for the Texas Legends basketball team, the minor league team for the Dallas Mavericks, and was quick on her feet. Since I am on the Personal Board of Directors for the President of the Legends, it only made sense to mentor Earlina. It was a win-win for both of us. Whenever we met for our mentoring sessions, we actually helped each other, because we each could offer our own perspective on a situation the other person was facing. Recently, Earlina became an entrepreneur herself, starting a yoga instruction business as well as a non-profit organization geared toward helping today's youth discover their purpose. She and I have a special bond, and I could not be more proud of her accomplishments.

One of the suggestions I always tell people about networking is to show up early. That way, you are already in the room and people will come up to you and start a conversation with you, instead of you having to walk into a room of people who are not yet your friends. By arriving early at another networking event, I met Karla, who was new to the group and was specifically looking to find a mentor. We met frequently and developed a strong bond. I helped her lay the groundwork for her PR business, and today she is a budding young entrepreneur herself. I am as proud of her as if she were my own daughter.

I don't believe in accidents, and I encourage you to embrace happenstance. Once you get on your feet as an entrepreneur, be open to the possibility of helping others do the same. You may not feel equipped to actively seek out a mentor/mentee relationship, but if the opportunity presents itself at a networking meeting or through mutual acquaintances, try to make yourself available. You may find that the relationship helps you in your business as much as it helps the up-and-comer you're advising.

Support Young Talent

After finding two mentees through happenstance, I decided to become an official mentor at the University of North Texas Professional Leadership Program. I knew I would be interacting with the top students at the university, who had to first earn a spot in the program. Each student is matched up to a mentor, and in my case, I struck gold. I was paired with a young woman named Shirley, whom I came to instantly love and respect.

As graduation nears, students have so many things to prepare for before they head out into the cold, cruel world, and Shirley and I discussed them all. We also went from talking about business and career planning to talking about the challenges that life brings, in general. On one very cold and rainy day, we met for lunch in a tiny town and the two of us sat and cried together as we shared about personal situations we each were facing. Our meetings had become a safe place, where no one was judged or criticized or rejected. And, our relationship continues to grow stronger both personally and professionally.

If you live near a college or university, find out whether a mentorship program is available. Many schools also offer internship opportunities through the career counseling office. Hiring a summer intern is a great way to get your feet wet as a mentor and provide valuable work experience for a student that can help them later in their career. You also get the benefit of having someone who is eager to learn working for you, often for a small stipend or low hourly rate.

Every one of the young women I have mentored as an entrepreneur, plus the dozens that I mentored throughout my insurance career, just needed a little help. Some may have needed it for a longer period of time than others, but they all needed someone who cared. Someone to help them get a leg up without judging their mistakes. Someone who believed in them when maybe, for that moment, they felt like no one else did.

Make an Impact

Sometimes, success isn't just about the money. It's about helping people. It's about giving back and it's about sharing information. One thing you don't expect, though, is how much you actually learn from the person you are mentoring. Sometimes the lessons you are sharing will speak volumes to you.

During my tenure in the insurance industry, as I became more successful and my name started to hit the company magazine, I received calls from other offices across the country asking whether I could give some advice to this woman, or could I convince this other woman that this was the right field, or could I talk another woman out of quitting. I recognized the value of that kind of guidance and helped out in any way I could. As I got promoted through the ranks and was an Agency Manager, I recruited many women onto my team—enough that made other offices sit up and take notice. I had the number one agent on my team who was right out of college and she actually received numerous awards at our annual event.

When I left the field to go into the corporate position, the calls for help didn't end. Even now, years later, I still get calls asking if I could just talk to another woman. It made me start to wonder how I could reach the next group of sales professionals and help them through some of the scary patches. Becoming a mentor as an entrepreneur was a natural next step.

Whether you are a man or a woman, and regardless of the industry you're in, you can help to nurture young talent and play a positive role in their professional journey. I always say, if just one woman had reached out her hand and offered to help me, my entire career would have been different.

My sweet mentees have taught me more about life than I could even explain. They all have a place in my heart and in my family. Every one of them was at my wedding and everyone that attended wanted to know their story and how we are all related. They are each on an exciting journey, the outcome of which is still yet to be determined.

Get Back to Basics

Last year, I met with my mentee Shirley, and I found myself giving her some solid advice—advice that I should have been following myself. She was nearing graduation, and she was facing a world of opportunities before her. She wanted to know, how do you choose one path when there are so many options in front of you?

The first question I asked her, that my business coach asked me some years ago, "If you could do anything you wanted and money, time and age would not be a factor and you could NOT fail, what would it be?" She had some definite answers, and as she was speaking, a name popped into my mind of someone I thought Shirley should connect with pronto. I made a call and quickly made introductions by phone. She was now starting her road map to get to her goals. We continued peeling back the onion and with each new layer, we came up with several ideas and strategies with agreed upon completion dates. As we wrote each item down on her calendar, the goal setting began.

Then it dawned on me—I needed the planning meeting just as much as she did. Although I was the savvy and seasoned entrepreneur in the relationship, our discussion helped me get back to basics and prompted me to assess my own business to ensure that I was still on track to reaching my goals, as well. Here is what I learned from our conversation:

1. **Write down your goals.** Understand that they

might need some adjusting and rearranging.

2. **Have someone to bounce things off of.** Your ideas might sound reasonable until you say them out loud. An objective person can add valuable insight.

3. **Never give up on your dreams.** Sometimes they may seem out of reach, but with some discussion and added resources they become crystal clear.

Remember, every day is the beginning of a new dream. Being an entrepreneur gives you the opportunity to realize your own vision and feel the remarkable satisfaction of making that vision a reality. And so, go forth! Focus on what is important to you and make those dreams come true for yourself and for others.

CONCLUSION

For most of my life, I have been an entrepreneur, whether as an independent contractor or running my own business. With one brief exception, I never had a weekly or bi-weekly paycheck, so my income depended solely on me. Providing for my children depended solely on me.

Selling in a Skirt was not my first venture as a business owner. In fact, I started my entrepreneurial journey selling Fuller Brushes. It was door-to-door sales in its truest sense. The first door I knocked on was my mom, and guess what? She said no! I couldn't believe it. How could your own mother say no to you when you are just starting out? Well, she did and for two valuable reasons. The first was because she wanted me to understand that just because someone likes you, they may not buy from you. The second was that she simply did not need what I was offering. Remember, it wasn't about me, the salesperson, it was about her, the customer.

Those are tough lessons to learn as a young, excited salesperson. But I had another lesson to learn. Even if someone doesn't buy from you, if they like you and trust you, they will share your information with others. Translation: referrals. My mom did give me some referrals, and my entrepreneurial career began right in front of me.

Over the years, I continued the pursuit of being my own boss until I decided to accept the challenge of being an employee in Corporate America. I love challenges and felt that I could cross "corporate job" off my bucket list. I fulfilled the responsibilities of the position and more. I earned the respect of most everyone in the company. But, the gig wasn't for me. I am an entrepreneur! I don't like to have that clock to punch. And, although having a regular paycheck was nice, it completely threw me off my game, because I had nothing extraordinary to reach for.

So, in the midst of a crashing economy, I resigned and started my own company. As I enter into my fourth year, I decided it was time to take the lessons I've learned and share them with other budding entrepreneurs, veteran entrepreneurs, and even those readers who just want to laugh and shake their head in disbelief, saying, "Nope, not for me." I wanted to share the great stories and the not-so-great ones, the mistakes I've made and the lessons learned. The way to share your message to the masses, and the keys for asking for help.

I'm no different from you.

I had an idea.

I took the plunge.

I figured out where to start.

I anticipated some setbacks.

But, I never gave up and I stayed the course...with a little flexibility and humor.

We all need someone to lean on and maybe, just maybe, I'm that person for you. If you want to be good, do it yourself. If you want to be great, do it together. Let's connect and stay connected. You can reach me at judy@sellinginaskirt.com.

I look forward to hearing about your journey, and how you are earning your fortune as an entrepreneur!

GET CONNECTED

For more information on Judy Hoberman, to schedule her to speak at your next event, or to have Judy develop a sales training program for your organization, please contact her through any of these media:

Website	www.sellinginaskirt.com
Facebook	facebook.com/sellinginaskirt
Twitter	@sellinginaskirt
Linkedin	http://linkd.in/judyh
Email	judy@sellinginaskirt.com